Preface

" And God has extracted you from the wombs of your mothers not knowing a thing, and He made for you hearing and vision and intellect that perhaps you would be grateful." **Noble Quran – 16 : 78**

All praise be to God Almighty who made me meet his chosen people through whom I have gained, assimilated and inculcated whatever I could in the past 25 years of my stay in Gulf.

I do believe that knowledge is power and it is obligatory on every one to share it with those who are deprived of it. Specially, with those millions who are under-privileged and do not have the means to acquire it. If we abstain from doing so, unarguably we, the learned, are committing a grave treachery unto our evolutionary spirit.

At this juncture, I remember with gratitude my mentor, philosopher and guide, Mr.Ali Abdulla Yateem, Chairman of Yateem Group for all the support he has rendered to me , without any reservations, in acquiring every bit of knowledge about optical field.

My association with the key customers had contributed tremendously in my personal growth. I thankfully remember them all. Every person in these organizations with whom I had associated myself in the past.

There is not enough space to mention the numerous names of the Optometrists, Sales staff and my own colleagues in J&J. A special thanks to my mentors whose leadership skills helped me achieve the desired goals.

Finally, a big thanks to Mr.Ali Bandor, Founder and Chief Editor of Eye Zone Magazine and his team, who helped me realize my skills as a writer.

I am presenting this book for the benefit of all, especially to those 'never say die' sales persons who live and breathe hope.

Happy Selling !!!

Mushtaq Ahmed

Table of Contents

1. Trust ! – How important is it in sales ?
2. Trust ! – Part 2
3. Aptitude. Attitude. Altitude
4. Know yourself. Do you ?
5. The individual and his insatiable appetite
6. Our needs define what we are
7. Our quest for skills
8. The fear factor
9. The price factor
10. Objections! Your Honor – Types of objections
11. Objections Sustained – Types of prospects
12. Sales person's magic wand
13. Closing the Sales.
14. Words that spell Magic
15. Advance Selling Skills Through NLP
16. Self-Improvement in The Light of NLP
17. Developing Your Communication Skills - NLP
18. Building Rapport With Your Customers – NLP
19. Special Offer – Optimism At 100% Discount
20. Things We Should Abstain From – In Sales
21. Port Folio Management
22. Relationship Dynamics With Colleagues
23. Communication Through Body Language – I & II
24. Customer Preferences and Choices – I to IV
25. The Leadership Game
26. Dare To Dream
27. Khaironomics – The Religion of Business
28. Khaironomics - Corporate Philanthropy
29. About The Author

Trust ! How Important Is It In Sales?

God does command you to render back your trust, to those to whom they are due." **Quran (4:58)**

It was a usual sunny morning in Dubai in the midst of July 1995. In most of the places in Gulf of Arabia, July is a terribly hot month. Just as you step out of your car, you would feel the gush of heat, as if you are in front of a furnace melting steel at 1600°. But Dubai's climate is different though. It is less hot perceptibly, around 45°, as compared to Riyadh or Kuwait, but irritatingly humid. No wonder, people lose patience quickly, even for trivial things.

I was in my office near the clock tower. I had just finished checking my emails, through Eudora, the first generation email software to download emails, and went to pick up the post mail from the reception.

I noticed a gentleman, attired like a Sales person, in his late twenties was standing near the reception desk enquiring. He was holding a plastic travel bag full of goods. He looked British and had a Londoner's accent.

"Hello! My name is Jim Walker", he introduced himself. "I wonder if I can speak to you for few minutes", he inquired in a mild tone. "We have ended up with a huge stock of this electric body massager", he disclosed showing me the specimen. "The market price of this item is Dhs.120/-. Since we wanted to get rid of the stock, we are now offering this item for Dhs.40/-, one third of the price. I appreciate if you might need one."

"Sorry, I don't." I politely refused shaking my head sideways.

"Perhaps you can help me to overcome my difficulties", he pleaded. "I have run out money since I lost my job and I am in deep financial mess. Moreover, I need to renew my residence visa", he added.

He touched my weak nerve. This guy wants to earn his buck and does not want to give up his self-esteem at the same time, I said to myself. I like people who struggle hard because that's the way I grew up, and I wanted to see myself in every human being, rather unfair you might say.

Being an expatriate in Gulf, I immediately realized what he was going through. One just cannot imagine losing the job and living here without a source of income, leave alone returning to the home country. I pulled out Dhs.40/- bills without a second thought and bought the electric body massager.

I had a pleasant feeling all day thinking that I had helped somebody who deserved to be helped. I can put the electric body massager to its right use during the weekends or perhaps, I can gift it to my mother who badly needed one. I patted my back for the good deed or rather a good deal done. Couple of days passed. I went roaming around Nasser Square area during the weekend. Whenever, I go to that Souq, it is irresistible for me to go the One Dirham Shop. It is such a fun to pick up novelties for one dirham or two Dirhams and give them to the children. Balash, as Arabs say.

Even though it was named One Dirham shop, I often find a whole lot of things which are valued at 10 Dirham and 20 Dirhams. One Dirham goods are a USP (Unique Selling Proposition) just to attract customers, I suppose.

I was looking at the tiny plastic flowers neatly tucked into a small flower vase. Something caught my attention suddenly; The Massager. There it was the same massager which I had bought in the office from the English guy. I picked it up out of curiosity and quickly saw the price sticker. It was printed 20 Dirhams. Half the price of what I had bought. "Hmmm…I got cheated", was my first thought. All that good feeling I had before started to vanish gradually even though it was just a negligible amount. I returned home consoling myself that it was not a big deal by paying 20 Dirhams more for somebody who deserved it. "Money is not a big deal, buddy", I said to myself. "What if he had taken advantage of my innocence?" I question myself.

As I entered my flat, I went straight to the cupboard to the see the massager which I had bought. I had not even removed the wrapper yet. Preserved it well for my mother I longed to see. No sooner I removed the wrapper there was another shocker. The groove at the head into which the massage plates need to be fitted had broken. I cannot use it anymore. Did he sell me a broken one? I wouldn't know. It was a big disappointment. "How could people make a life out cheating like this?" I asked myself never to be answered.

At that very point, I promised myself never to buy from an outdoor sales person again. Never to be cheated again; never to be the same gullible innocent buyer again.

This reiterates the fact that the first criteria for Selling are Trust. "Selling should be based on relationships not on transactions. "Building relationships is a practice and not a process" as put by Charles Green. Therefore, Trust is product of relationships between the buyer and seller. It is quite a human thing. Beyond the products you sell, beyond the brands you display and beyond the discounts you offer.

I have heard of so many stories from my friends, relatives and the people in the market as to how they had been cheated while buying a product. Not one of them had returned to buy from the same shop let alone the same sales person.

My friends in Saudi Arabia say it is so hard to sell something new in Saudi as generally customers do not trust the sales persons there. They stick to the old habits or old products, unwilling to change. Every time a sales person suggests something new, the customer gives a suspicious look at him. A kind of 'don't trap me' frowns. This has not happened overnight, I am sure. Losing Trust is not like losing body weight. It happens quite fast. It affects you quite fast. You feel dejected, disappointed and betrayed. One Salesman's betrayal leads to loss of trust in the whole organization. No religion has missed this point in emphasizing it. Because honesty and trust are such a vital part of our spiritual make up. They are ingrained in the human psyche. Between two people, it is a two-way street. It cannot exist by itself. There has to be another party. It cannot be that one person cheats another and still expects the other to trust him.

Let's see what the religious scriptures say. The Bible says: "Whoever can be trusted with very little can also be trusted with much, and whoever is dishonest with very little will also be dishonest with much." Luke 16:10

Somebody has to take the first step though, and it's got to be you; - the Sales Person in this case. If you're interested in developing a relationship, you have to be willing to take the first risk to offer something up. It's a TITO – GIGO. You put Trust Into somebody you get Trust Out, likewise you put Garbage in – you get Garbage out.

I'm not upset that you lied to me, I'm upset that from now on I can't believe you – **Friedrich Nietzsche**

Trust – Part 2

Just when I was thinking of penning on the next topic, I asked myself if I had discussed enough on **Trust**. I owe you all an answer to this question, "How important is Trust in sales?"

A little girl and her father were crossing a bridge. The father was a bit scared so he asked his little daughter, "Baby, please hold my hand so that you don't fall into the river." The little girl said, "No, dad. You hold my hand." "What's the difference?" asked the puzzled father. "There's a BIG difference," replied the little girl.

"If I hold your hand and something happens to me, chances are that I may let your hand go. But if you hold my hand, I know for sure that no matter what happens, you will never let my hand go."

In any relationship, the essence of trust is not in its bind, but in its bond. So hold on to your customer who trusts you rather than expecting them to hold on to you.

The very reason I wish to emphasize this topic at length is because of its enormous importance at the frontline when you are dealing with new clients every day, sowing the seeds of trust and at the same time, help the sown seeds to germinate. What I mean by that is your efforts to build trust start to the results.

The Three Pillars of Trust

Dr. Duwain Tway defines trust as, "the state of readiness for unguarded interaction with someone."

The first pillar, **capacity for trusting** means that your total life experiences have developed your current capacity and willingness to risk trusting others.

The second pillar, **perception of competence** is made up of your perception of your ability and the ability of others with whom you work to perform competently.

The third **perception of intentions**, is your perception that the actions, words, or decisions are motivated to mutually serve the buyer and the seller.

In my two decades of Gulf life, the Trust factor has played a huge role in making or breaking lives, leave aside careers.

The most trusted employees who had spent their life time in the same company, had been denigrated to ZEROES from HEROES and eventually consigned to oblivion or jailed in some cases.

Friends, as a matter of fact, most of are here in this region as expatriates who want to make a living; whether we like it or not, whether we have come here voluntarily or were forced by compulsions. Let's make the best out of this situation.

Every word uttered about the product "superiority", be it Titanium or Titus; every promise made to deliver, be it progressives or prescription tints, results in a transaction at the counter level which needs to be handled with utmost efficacy and professionalism.

Thus, leaving an indelible imprint on the customers mind. The end result is… happy customers. The happier customers are, the more loyal they are. *That's all ye know on earth…. And ye need to know.*

At the end of the day, this is what is going reflect on your attitude and distinctly identify you in the crowd as *Mia Bil Mia*, meaning Hundred Percent Trustworthy.

"Without trust, selling becomes hollow and dead as the empty shell of last year's nut.
With trust, selling becomes life itself." **Anonymous**

Attitutude. Aptitude. Altitude

Beyond the stars there are worlds more. Our quest remains to be tested yet more.
This existence alone does not matter. There are boundless journeys yet more
You are the falcon, your passion is flight. And you have skies more to transcend with delight. Lose not yourself in the cycle of day and night.
Within your reach are feats bright

Dr. Allama Iqbal, the legendary urdu poet of 20th century had written the above poem which has given me the wings to fly all my life.

We all wish to reach our desired altitude in our respective fields. We strive to acquire the desired capability (aptitude) to achieve this altitude. But why do only few of us succeed? The answer to this question lies in one's own attitude towards life.

Attitude, my friends, is an inner feeling followed by outward disposition. "The best and the most beautiful things in the world cannot be seen or touched but are felt in the heart", said Hellen Keller.

Attitude exists within you until you breathe last. Whether you like it or hate it, you mask it or reveal it. It's like a mind's paint brush; it can either be used like a Picasso to paint 'The Dream' or like a street urchin to deface the wall.

The unarguable point here is that it exists in us, along with our flesh and bones. Sometimes on the scowl or frown explicit. Sometimes, within the deep folds of the subconscious mind.

Like we have a choice to transform our blood into good blood or bad blood, we can also change our attitude into good attitude or bad attitude. In other words, it's either 'Positive Attitude' or 'Negative Attitude'.

Let me make this clearer.

There was a dolphin trainer who got his dolphin to talk. This dolphin became one of its kind as it started entertain everyone by its quick, curt and pertinent replies. The dolphin trainer wanted to share his accomplishment with his friends. He invited his close friend for the show.

He asked the dolphin, "Hi! Dolly, what's up?" to which it replied, "Cool Johnny. Life is fun." He queried few more times and pat came the replies from his Dolly.

The trainer was expecting his friend to compliment him for this amazing feat but never saw him open his mouth. The show finished and they were returning home together.

He asked his friend about the dolphin show, his friend replied, "Yeah. I thought your Dolly would sing, but she didn't." What an attitude! Ridiculously unsavory.

Let's simplify what 'Positive Attitude' means. Ask yourself the following questions:

Are you a happy person?

Are you happy at your work same as you are at home ?

Do you enjoy every moment of being in the showroom whether it be in a shopping mall or in the street ?

How do you feel while leaving the showroom? Is it like "Thank God the day is finished!" or do you have the eagerness to return soon next morning to compensate for the lost opportunities in sales?

How different are you compared to sales people in the market? How passionate are you to learn more about silver halide components in photochromic lenses work, or the benefits of progressives for computer users?

Have you ever been inquisitive about Computer Vision Syndrome and made it easier for your customers to know. Wouldn't your customers respect you for this information if you share?

Lastly and most importantly, have you ever asked yourself before you slept, "What did I do differently today to improve myself and at the same time help my patients' vision get better.

Have a look around you, ladies and gentlemen. Life is not just counting your commission money or waiting for the day to end. The retail showroom chains which surround you were not created in a day.

The Chairmen or the CEOs of these huge empires were and are ordinary people like us. Even today if you happen to meet them, you will be overwhelmed by their simplicity and dedication. No surprise to see them talking to customers explaining how to wear Reading Glasses or fixing the nose pads.

It's their positive attitude that has driven them. And the dreams they saw with their eyes wide open that had helped them to scale those heights.

> *Today is the day for you to progress. There's something productive you can do to improve your world. It may not seem like much, and yet it can make a big difference. You can waste this moment or you can use it. There's a world of difference between those two simple choices. Though you may not immediately achieve anything stunning or momentous, still you can achieve right here and right now. And once you've achieved, you will feel so good that you'll jump right in and achieve again.... And again. This is your day and this is your life. It's happening right now, and you can do something wonderful with it. Here is your chance to make a little progress, so .... DO IT.*
> **Ralph Marston**

Know Yourself. Do You ?

"What's in a name? That which we call a rose by any other name would smell as sweet"

Thus spoke Juliet to Romeo Montague in Shakespeare's lyrical tale. We have heard this expression quite often, didn't we ?

What's your name asked Jack Brown as he entered the shop. The gentleman behind the desk replied happily, "My name is John". Ram or Robert or Rabinder Singh, could by anything.

Ask yourself this question as to why do you call yourself that name. Is it just because your parents named you or is it because your friends call you so or perhaps the birth certificate has your name written on it. Irrespective of all the above, the very fact that you call yourself Ram or Robert is because **You Believe That Is How You Need To Be Called.**

No matter where you are and how you are. Even if you had jumped out of a burning aeroplane and landed in the midst of Sahara desert and had no document to prove, you would still call yourself the very name that you believe in and loved to be called after.

Apparently, the next questions that arise are - What does your name signify and what does it reflect to others. Does your name signify trust, honesty, truthfulness, reliability, straight forwardness, simplicity and so on. So much so that it becomes the epitome of all virtues and good things in life. Eventually, becoming 'a name' that would be sought after among the people you live in. Rejoice Boy! you have now become a brand name.

Ask yourself why is it that in a street of ten physicians, that one particular General Practitioner always has his clinic full of patients to the brim. Why is that Abu Mohammed barges into the showroom and looks only for Maher Dibbie and does not bother to acknowledge anybody else's smile. That's because a brand foot print has been created in the mind of the consumer or patient.

What is a brand then ?

It is all about how different and distinguished you are the midst of the crowd. As they say, either you may buy a car or you may buy a Mercedez. The difference is huge. The difference is real. Therefore, be a Merck yourself.

Total Quality Person

While I was working in Johnson & Johnson Vision Care, we all had gone to attend the EMA meeting in Barcelona, Spain. On the last night of the sales conference, we all usually get together for the Gala Dinner. Such conferences, without any doubt, are well planned and well managed by big companies.

Strange food appears on your plate with stranger names. Gougeres, Kalamata Olive Tapenade, Coquilles, Chicken Schnitzel. I still remember the grilled salmon served during this meeting fresh from the Besos river.

As we approached our table, I saw a tall American who had arrived earlier than us. He must have been feeling hungry, I thought. He came forward and stretched his hand to greet me.

" Hello!, my name is Dave Smith", he introduced himself.

"Oh, Hi! My name is Mushtaq", I grinned coming of out of my nutshell. I must confess at this juncture that I have a huge problem in my personality while meeting people. Ninety nine out hundred times, I am not the one to stretch my hand and introduce myself to other people. This still exists. But once the ice breaks, I am a different person altogether.

Now about Dave, I though he must be some sales representative, Account Manager, as we dignify his designation. Hence must be eager to mingle with us to know about Dubai perhaps, I thought to myself.

" So, where are you from ?", I asked him casually.

"Well, I am from United States. I thought it will be a good opportunity to meet you guys and learn from your success stories", he added.

" Oh! Of course, we will be glad to do that", I answered. "By the way, what do you there in our company in States, Dave", I queried.

" I am assigned as Vice President-Sales", responded Dave calmly.

For a while, my hands became cold and numb and the color of my face must have definitely turned weird. Even in the wildest my dreams, I never imagined somebody from such a top position would sit along with us and chat so casually. He was simplicity personified.

Thereafter, these incidences became a norm than an exception in J&J.

Great organizations are not evaluated by the working conditions they exhibit or remunerations they offer. They are measured by the attitudes and relationships demonstrated by the employees towards each other. They are represented by 'Total Quality People' at every front of the organization. Especially, at those fronts where substantial interaction takes place with clients.

There are umpteen times I have come across so many people at the sales front who would not bother to establish even a simple eye contact with their customers and let along throwing a plastic smile at them.

Someone once approached Blaise Pascal, the famous French philosopher and said, "if I had your brains, I would be a better person'. Pascal replied, " Be a better person first, you will have my brains."

If in the last few years you haven't discarded a major opinion about yourself or acquired a new one, check your pulse. You may be dead.

~**Gelett Burgess**

Our Needs Define What We Are

"O Adam! dwell thou and thy wife in the Garden, and enjoy (its good things) as you wish: but approach not this tree, or you run into harm and transgression." Then began Satan to whisper suggestions to them, bringing openly before their minds all their shame that was hidden from them (before): he said: "Your Lord only forbade you this tree, lest you should become angels or such beings as live forever." **-The Noble Quran –Al Araf –Verse -19**

Adam and Eve (pbut) felt the need to live forever and transgressed. Man since creation was ingrained with needs and wants. Obama needed his oratorical skills to win over his friends and enemies. Putin needed the hang glider to fly along with the Siberian cranes and prove himself as an animal lover.

People in Gulf prefer SUVs instead of Corollas and Civics to overcome the challenges on highways. Thus the needs which exist in humans are voluminous. We need General Air conditioners, Mont Blanc Pens, Armani Suits, Chanel Sunglasses, Samsung S9s and the remote control car keys, if possible with a bling.

Abu Badr walked into an optical store in Jamaiyya (co-operative stores in Kuwait are called Jamaiyyas). Until yesterday, everything seemed ok for him while he drove his car, a recently bought Mercedes Maybach G650. He felt suddenly that his eyes were no longer co-operating. Associated with the vision problem was the slight headache appearing every now and then.

He had consulted his physician who suggested him to have his eyes checked. What the heck it could be, thought Abu Badr. He had just crossed his 40th year.

" Taal Dactoora, I need an eye exam", he requested with his hoarse sandy voice. Lady Optometrists in Kuwait get the luxury of being addressed as 'Doctoora'.

The lady optometrist exhibited all her expertise to perform a detailed eye examination and came out with the prescription which indicated hyperopic astigmatism with presbyopia. She handed over the prescription to Abu Badr with an obligatory Kabayan smile and comforted him not to worry, reassuring that their sales staff are competent enough to address all his issues.

"Give me good discount, I have only 100 dinars (US$.350 approx) in my pocket", commanded Abu Badr authoritatively. "And make it fast, I have to go to Dewaniya".

Abu Badr was sold a branded frame with first generation progressive lenses to suit his budget just to impress him that he had been charged less so that he could have the "Balaash" feeling.

This scenario could have been made different. All it needs is an extra effort. It needs the Sales Front to walk that extra mile, to work that extra hour, to make that extra buck and to climb that extra step of ladder in life. Not an easy task though. But highly rewarding. As you retire, you may look back to see your life full of achievements and self-satisfaction.

If we analyze the situation above, a little more of knowing the life style of Abu Badr, questioning and understanding his needs would have definitely helped in selling a premium high-end frame worth more than US$.3000/- with Poly-carbonate lenses embedded with Transition Photochromic technology with latest Blue Filter Anti-reflection coating either from Crizal or Zeiss or Nikon or Seiko.

Funniest thing to see is how on earth somebody would dispense basic progressive lenses to a customer who has the capacity to spend at least 1000 dollars a day. Wouldn't Abu Badr be loving to have the latest blue filter progressive lenses with a high end Cartier or Maybach or solid gold Silhouette to his friends in Diwaniya. And what's more, he would have referred your outlet to a couple of his friends too.

Man's mind is a composition of needs and desires. His wants are infinite in variety and number. Some wants are natural, for example foods, air, clothing and shelter without which existence of man's life is not possible. Similarly wants vary from individual to individual and they multiply as he grows and get civilized.

He is never completely satisfied and hence there is no end to human wants. As one want is satisfied another want will crop up to take its place and thus evolves a never ending cycle of wants. As we are in the business of selling, let us identify those needs and wants and cater to them to serve our mutual interests.

You need only six Ws and an H to perfectly sell an aeroplane – Grace and Noble

The Individual And His Insatiable Appetite

The color of the eyes, and the innocence they behold; the glow on the lip-stick, and the truth spelt by lips; the complexion of hands, and the help offered to the needy; the golden anklets worn on feet, and the brave steps taken to climb the mountains; the palpitations of the Heart and the Purity of its content are all nothing but the Power of the Individuality.

Anonymous

In the earlier article, we had discussed that our needs and wants define what we are. Then we stressed upon the importance of acquiring and developing those skills, more importantly related to questioning, to find out the needs and wants of our customers so that we can adequately offer them appropriate solutions.

The Power of Individuality

We are individuals. We exist in this world as distinct and separate entities even though we may be vociferous in expressing our belief that man is a social being and invite fellow humans to join the same group, wear the same cap or sport the same tie.

At the end of the day, every one of us is different. Our beliefs are different. Our passions, tastes, likes, dislikes, whims and fancies are all different based on how we perceive this world from our own axis, our own meridians. It all ends up to " I " and "what's in it for me".

This comprises of our inner world which is embedded in our subconscious mind. To elevate our self from "I" and merge it with the ocean of "We" is a different esoteric topic which philosophers call 'the evolution to higher consciousness.

Apparently, our individuality is based on self-preservation, differentiation, dominance and upward mobility. To sustain these attributes every individual behaves in a particular way that is distinct and different than others. The sales person in you need to identify these areas of differentiation.

Constructive Interference

Interference is a characteristic of light according to Wave Optics. When the waves superimpose in such a way that their maxima and minima correspond with each other, the resultant intensity is greater than the sum of the intensities due to separate waves. This is known a Constructive Interference, which students of Optometry have been trying to understand. What this really means is one plus one is equal to three or may be more.

The speed of light is known to be 300,000 km/sec. And light, as we know, contains tiny particles called photons and it also travels in the form of waves and as well as straight lines.

The individual's thought process is faster than the speed of light. Its locomotion and ingredients will be as challenging as Wave Theory to understand. It might appear wavy at times it will look very straight.

As an Eye Care professional, never have pre-fixed notions about your customers by following Edward De Bono or Ned Herrmann about characterizing the individual's behavior. You might end up having a rude shock. Being at the sales front is like swimming in the ocean. You may encounter a ferocious shark to escape or have the opportunity to dance with the dolphin. They both are inhabitants of the sea but their traits are different.

When Fatima and Sara, the twin sisters approach you for a spectacle frame, one might go for a glittering golden-rimmed frame studded with stones, the other might prefer a rimless titanium in matt black. As you explore their mind further, you may know they both fancy to be Angelina Jolie or Nancy Ajram. And therefore they need cosmetic enhancements to reflect their mindset.

A few stones on the temple may be or a graded color on their sunglasses or perhaps prescription lenses with mirror coating. The opportunities to sell more always exist because of the individual's insatiable appetite to have more.

Mirroring Effect

Physiologist Vittorio Gallese and Leo Fogassi of the Rizzolatti research team were working with Macaque monkeys researching their brain. One of the researchers was in the lab and was eating ice cream while one of the research monkeys was still hooked up to the research machines.

That triggered the area of the brain of the monkey as if she too was doing the exact same thing of eating ice cream. The researchers came up with the mane of mirror neurons to label this part of the brain. The result of the eating mishap was that the researchers found that monkeys and humans see themselves doing what you do to some degree or another.

A successful salesperson should have the necessary mirroring skills to influence people psychologically. This can only happen when you know what is in in the depth of your customer's mind. Thus you may synergize the needs and the solutions with greater effect and enhance the resultant output like it is done in Constructive Interference. Do it. I know you will from now on.

"You have your way. I have my way. As for the right way, the correct way, and the only way, it does not exist."

Friedrich Nietzsche

Our Quest for Skills

All Scripture is inspired of God and beneficial for teaching, for reproving, for setting things straight, for disciplining in righteousness, that the man of God may be fully competent, completely equipped for every good work. Timothy 3:16, 17.

Its MIDO time in March. Most of us in the optical industry know what it is. For those who don't.. it is the most happening event in Italy every year exhibiting a range of optical products.

More than 50000 visitors call on with their eyes and ears wide open to take a glance, touch and feel the newest products that are showcased and sign deals with a smile.

And they all come with a common thought and a question, "What's new this time ?". Its not surprising to hear the same question being asked by the optometrists when visited by the sales representatives in their clinics or the customers to the front line staff in showrooms, "What's new today ?"

There is an urge ingrained and inherent in us to ask questions. When we were children, we had asked our parents as to how do the aeroplanes fly or what does the old lady on the moon supposed to be doing. And that urge persisted as we grew older and our curiosity led us to know, ask and gather every wee bit of information we had wanted until we were told rudely to shut up and stop asking questions – which eventually had stifled and killed the Einstein in us.

Octavio Paz, the famous Mexican poet said, "Man is a being who asks questions. From the time we are born we begin to ask questions . . . It might even be said that mankind's history is the history of questions and answers that we men have formulated."

So the best way to kick start our quest for acquiring the questions skills is by asking 'Why'. Good heavens! what a revolution this interrogative had created. Newton asked "Why does the apple fall ?, " and here we have the reason for gravity. Humpry Davy questioned "Why is it so dark at night", we have got the Electric bulb glowing in our bedroom. When Janssen asked why can't we see the invisible creatures, we now have got a microscope to detect microbial keratitis.

Thus people kept their urge alive to ask questions and find answers and unraveled the mysteries and unearthed the treasures whereby we started to enjoy the benefits of having cars, bikes, air conditioners, laptop, emails, blackberries, shades, spectacles, contact lenses and what not.

Let's develop our Questioning Skills

Let's give a proper shape to our curiosity. When the customer enters our showroom, we are ready to throw our customary smile, "Hello Ma'm, how are you?" along with this the day starts with a nice ice breaker.

Questioning skills help us to build rapport with our customers by demonstrating our interest in them. They also help us to find their visible and hidden needs. Most importantly, they help us to motivate the customers to buy.

Open Questions which start with What, Which, Why, When, Where, Who and How are very helpful to explore the needs of the customers which sometimes they themselves are not aware of.

An open question such as "What have you been using in the past?" can reveal customer's likes and preferences.

"How did you feel using that X brand of frames or contact lens ?" can divulge customer's real life experiences.

" How has the problem of not seeing distant objects affected you?" can help the customer share his pain with you.

An appropriate empathetic expression on your face can definitely strengthen your relationship with Ms.Beth or Mr.Belmando.

In the end, what we would like to achieve at the sales counter or inside the clinic is to get the customer speak his or her heart out so that we narrow down his or her needs and offer him or her the appropriate solution.

Ask yourself if you have ever bothered to learn the questioning techniques. If you were ever concerned to ask your manager to help you improve your questioning skills. This would have resulted in eventually improving your overall sales. If you had ever questioned yourself what you are and where you need to be. If didn't, do it today.

The important thing is not to stop questioning. Curiosity has its own reason for existing. **-Albert Einstein**

How Contact Lenses Can Change Customers' Perception About Life

All we have to believe with is our senses, the tools we use to perceive the world: our sight, our touch, our memory. If they lie to us, then nothing can be trusted. And even if we do not believe, then still we cannot travel in any other way than the road our senses show us; and we must walk that road of the world to the end.

Neil Gaiman, American Gods

June the 2nd was an unusual day in Chennai. I was reclining on Sunday evening on the outskirts of the metro when I heard the sudden pattering sound on the window sill. Indeed I was surprised; it was raining. It was such a pleasant sight to see and feel the monsoon in June in Chennai to give the inhabitants some relief from the humid and muggy weather. For a person like me who has stayed all his life in Gulf, rain in Rahma, mercy from God. Even the slightest relief from the current plight looks like a huge favor for us.

Effect Of Contact Lenses on People's Lives

Around two decades ago, my friend Dr.Patel asked me once, " why are contact lenses named so". As a novice in the contact lens industry, I replied to him in the smartest way I could. "Dr.Patel, you are the best person to teach me about it". I am sure, he must have felt flattered.

"Contact Lenses are named so because they are in contact with the cornea", he answered.

Those were the days we had only that much of information. Contact lenses are not only in contact with the cornea but also very much in contact with the tear-film, a fact which has been largely ignored since the early period of their (r)evolution. Besides there were only few options available on the shelf in those days. Minus Lenses (for Myopes) and Plus Lenses (for Hyperopes), the rest were custom-made or Rx which took ages to manufacture and deliver.

Today, there are abundant options, a huge range, plenty of stock on the shelf and various choices. Imagine that an astigmat with as high as -3.25D cylindrical power can be fitted and dispensed with in no time.

How to Triple your Transaction Value Per Customer

Nevertheless, the opportunity to increase transactional value per customer at the sales counter is at times more than triple.

Firstly, most of the contact lens wearers do feel the need of having a pair of spectacles, just in case they need it on occasion.

Secondly, the psychological impact of contact lenses is so enormous that customers feel an ardent desire to try every model of sunglasses as they probe showroom shelf.

Thirdly, contact lens wearers who wear transparent lenses, might opt for colored variants on occasions. There are even situations that the weekly wearers choose daily disposables while travelling.

Last but not the least, by introducing contact lenses to your customers, you bear witness to change as to how they look at themselves and the world around them.

There is an enormous boost in patients' self-esteem. Enormous freedom which remained elusive. They look so natural as they deserve to be. No more branding of 'the lady with the specs" or "the boy with four eyes".

Now, your patients look real, original, full of confidence to take on the world head on, to play the football without the fear, to smile at their friends without confusing them whether they are looking at them or somebody else.

Thus you are only enhancing their loyalty, because you have helped them change the way they have been perceiving about themselves and the world at large.

And Loyalty is product of Happiness which eventually results in regular business and what more - you will get referred customers too.

How to suggest contact lenses ?

Let's simplify the process of suggesting contact lenses to the patients. It is a fact of life that most patients spend maximum time interacting with the frontline staff.

At first, establish rapport with your customers/patients to gain their trust and confidence so that they can speak to you freely.

Ask simple questions at an opportune moment.

'Madam/Sir, May I ask your opinion if you don't mind ? What do you feel about contact lenses as a vision care option?

The positive answers will immediately lead to trials.

" Yes, I would be more happy to try them".

The negative answers will reflect their perception of fear embedded deep in their mind because of the bad experience they have had in the past.

Some might have had red eyes by wearing low quality devices, some might feel contact lenses are expensive besides the fact that the average spend on contact lenses is cheaper than the coffee people consume every day. Some might assume the sharp nail of the practitioner might pierce their eye.

A good way forward is to capture the data of the number of customers to whom you had suggested contact lenses and how many had declined the offer and the reasons behind it.

Objections to wear contact lenses are only ' Buying Signals'. All you now have to learn is to overcome those objections. Companies like Johnson and Johnson Vision, Alcon and Bausch and Lomb are offering immense professional support for you to learn these aspects.

The result of this proactivity will be for you to relish. Be The Change You Want To See.

If the doors of perception were cleansed everything would appear to man as it is, infinite. For man has closed himself up, till he sees all things through narrow chinks of his cavern.

William Blake

The Fear Factor

Where the mind is without fear and the head is held high, Where knowledge is free, Where the world has not been broken up into fragments, By narrow domestic walls , Where words come out from the depth of truth, Where tireless striving stretches its arms towards perfection, Where the clear stream of reason has not lost its way into the dreary desert sand of dead habit , Where the mind is led forward by thee ,Into ever-widening thought and action , Into that heaven of freedom, my Father, let my country awake.
Rabindranath Tagore

What is Fear? Fear is our body's reaction to a stressful stimulus which leads to a fight or flight response. As a result, a frightened person exhibits signs of fear such as nail biting, fearful look, trembling, keeping hands under the chin, lack of eye contact, speechlessness, forgetfulness etc. eventually leading to all sort involuntary errors at work place.

The basis of fear in a sales person could be inadequacies of certain factors such as lack of product knowledge, inability to justify price, lack of command over language, inability to understand customer needs, inability to provide appropriate solutions to the problems stated by the customer etc. we can go on and on.

Customers too exhibit a lot of fear for various reasons such as bad publicity about the store or the product, lack of rapport with the sales person, lack of factual evidence to try new products, being cheated at sales point during previous occasions etc. – once bitten twice shy you might say.

The first step to eliminate fear is to pinpoint it. As a child I used to fear darkness. I used to fear jinns and ghost wearing the blanket of blackness. That phobia persisted even as I had grown up.

One fine night, I decided to overcome my fear. I grabbed a little torch and walked into the jungle of Kannivakkam near Guduvancheri on the outskirts of Chennai. It dawned on me on that moonless night that those ghosts existed only in my mind.

<u>Underline</u> where exactly you have the problem. Is lack of knowledge about the product itself or is it about the way to position and sell it. Is it about its features, advantages and benefits etc. or is it about knowing your customers or end users.

Create a check list of what you should know that is relevant to your business and the way to derive that information. This act will build enormous confidence in you and eliminate your anxiety.

Justifying the price of the products needs confidence and courage again. Consumers these days are habituated asking for discounts because they feel the same product could be available elsewhere for a lesser price. Needless to say that most of the products are available online at a reduced price.

Genuineness of the product and exceptional service are key the factors that could alleviate the fear in customer's mind. At the end of the discussion, deliver that winning punch-line.

"Ma'am, how much do you spend for your coffee per day or on fuel for your car or on your mobile phone bill per month. The total cost of these lenses/frames etc will be lesser than what you spend on those things on an yearly basis."

Buttress the punch-line with credibility. "Ours is a fifty year old authorized retail showroom and we are reputed for our service and after care." The stronger the confidence building measures the faster the riddance of fear.

Have you prepared yourself to overcome fear

A blind boy sat on the steps of a building with a hat by his feet. He held up a sign which said: 'I am blind, please help...' There were only a few coins in the hat. A man was walking by took the sign, turned it around, and wrote some words. He put the sign back so that everyone who walked by would see the new words.

Soon the hat began to fill up. A lot more people were giving money to the blind boy. That afternoon the man who had changed the sign came to see how things were. The boy recognized his footsteps and asked, 'Were you the one who changed my sign this morning? What did you write?' The man said, 'I only wrote the truth. I said what you said but in a different way.' What he had written was: 'Today is a beautiful day and I cannot see it.'

"Disability is a matter of perception. If you can do just one thing well, you're needed by someone.", says Martina Navratilova. If fear is your disability conquer it. Lack of confidence leads to lack of credibility. And the end result is slack in performance, in other words lack of business.

Practice is the magic word to overcome your short-comings. Do they say 'practice *maketh a man perfect*'.

How much do you do practice your sales call before you meet the customer. If your management takes an evaluation about your sales efficiency, it is most likely that many of you will pass only with average ratings. Its time to leave aside all these misconceptions about self and take the Goliath head on. Get the real David out of you. Yes you can, certainly. Battles are won in mind before they are fought on the field.

So what is needed now do you think.

Rather than running away or controlling or suppressing or putting any other resistance -- Understand fear; that means, watch it, learn about it, come directly into contact with it. We are to learn about fear, not how to escape from it.

J Krishnamurti

The Price Factor

*" When his heart forsakes fairness and
his deeds turn depraved,
A man realizes deep within himself, "I am ruined".*
Verse : 116 , Thirukkural

Abu Marwan had a sleepless night. "How could he do this to me, he thumped the mattress. " I had been purchasing only from him for the past 10 years", he grumbled.

Abu Marwan had bought a Rado True Thinline Diamonds wrist watch from his trusted sales person Bilal with whom he had been dealing regularly for a decade. Last night when he was at the Diwaniya, a traditional get-together in Arabia, he was excited to ostentatiously display his 'black beauty' to his friends. Every one of them were eager to know about its price and from whom he had bought that precious jewel.

Eyes ogled out and compliments poured in from everyone alike. But his dearest friend Abu Waleed had different thoughts. "Habibi, you have bought it expensive. I can get you the same thing cheaper by thirty percent. Moreover, you need to be sure if it is original", he whispered in his ear.

Abu Marwan kept staring at his watch, punching the pillow all night. The thought that he might have been cheated bothered him. He stayed awake for so long and never knew when he had dozed off.

When he woke up, expectedly the first thing Abu Marwan would do was to rush to Bilal. He had all the questions in his mind to tear the poor salesman apart. He barged into the showroom and started to fire his salvos incessantly.

Bilal calmly heard him to empty his barrage of questions. He escorted him into the manager's cabin. By the time Abu Marwan left the showroom, he was a changed man with a smile on his face, fully convinced and looking at his watching again and again treasuring his possession.

What could have happened in the cabin do you think?

The manager of the showroom, Faris, answered all his questions with amazing confidence and audacity. He showed him the difference between the original Rado and the counterfeit one. The number on the ETA movement, the font and print, the nickel plating etc. He was assuaged that all authorized showrooms quote the same retail price and if he finds the price cheaper, he could have this piece as a gift. And most importantly, Bilal confided how he had saved that last piece for Abu Marwan to honor their relationship.

All this could have been done at the time of purchase as well to save themselves from embarrassment. Nevertheless, with so much of reassurance, Abu Marwan felt that he has not been cheated at all and in fact may have got more than its value.

The difference between price and value

The difference between price and value is as big as you realize between 'buying the product' or 'being sold'. Most customers buy the products for their value rather than the price.

Have your ever found a patient having heart attack bargaining the fees with the surgeon. He or she is willing to pay a fortune as long as his or her life is saved. Oscar Wilde said "A cynic is someone who knows the price of everything and the value of nothing".

Quite often you might have customers who are so keen to get the best price out of you. What could be the reason behind this ? Showrooms on high street or shopping malls have few issues as regards pricing is concerned. These price points require persistent efforts to enhance value.

Defining Value

According to Oxford dictionary, value means the worth of something compared to the price paid or asked for it. In the earlier article we discussed about contact lenses. Even though the customers purchase them for about 25 U.S. dollars, the value perceived by them is enormous and cannot be quantified due the benefits they experience.

Value arises from what the product does and how it benefits the customer. Therefore, it is essential to understand the customer's perspective as to how they evaluate a certain product.

Price is just a number to make merchandize profitable for the business. Price is the buyer's input; value results in longer-term effect. When the benefits outnumber the price the buyer pays, the solution you provide has great value to him.

When people are bargaining the price, there is a perceived lack of fairness behind the amount mentioned on the product; that is, they feel they are paying more than what they are receiving, in some way.

So how can you get your prospects to look beyond up-front price and concentrate on the value of your product?

That can only happen when you help your customers realize the enormous benefits that your product offers. That could be about the brand equity, the number of filters and their benefits, the amount of UV protection, the tensile strength or the thinness of the lens, the proportionate increase in visual acuity, increase in field of vision or reduction in distortion, the advantages of materials like titanium; you can go on and on.

Thus you may emphasize and engage your prospect to focus on the value rather than price. The prospect has to think about the long-term benefits of dealing with you rather than just highlighting the price differentials.

That would result in 'I have bought it' feeling with the fist punching in the air rather than " I was sold by him" feeling with the fist banging on the desk. That would result in your selling enjoyable, is it not ?

The major value in life is not what you get. The major value in life is what you become.
Jim Rohn

Objection, Your Honor

Everyone has the right to freedom of thought and expression. This right includes freedom to seek, receive, and impart information and ideas of all kinds, regardless of frontiers, either orally, in writing, in print, in the form of art, or through any other medium of one's choice.

Article 13 – American Convention on Human Rights

A court room is probably the only place where were hear the word 'objection' objectionably repetitive. Objections could be counter-opinions of a person not willing to accept your part of the argument.

Let me share with you this joke. The judge sat on his chair to begin the court proceedings. The lawyers positioned themselves. As the witness stood in the witness box, the judge said, `You seem to be visibly distressed, is there anything that matters?'.

"Well, your Honour," said the witness clearing his throat, "I swore to tell the truth, the whole truth and nothing but the truth, but every time I try, some lawyer objects."

What are Sales Objections ?

A Sales Objection is a reason or an argument by the buyer for not buying your product. On the other hand, this may be treated as a buying signal. A buyer could put forth a list of objections upon clearing the same, he could become your happy customer.

Beware of the difference between Objection and Rejection. A buyer might disguise Rejection in the form of Objection. In which case, whatever you do or say or bend your back to please the customer, you would only hear him say a flat "No" to your offer.

How to handle objections ?

Most objections in every trade get repeated and it important to learn how to handle them. The following are the ways to do it:

Realize and Understand :

Do not let the customer's objections hurt your ego. Most sales people take objections personally and wind up the sales call then and there.

A better way to handle objections is to 'hear patiently, realize and understand'. " The price of same model of Armani, Gucci or Prada is high as compared to other shops in the market, why is that ? "- Price objections are common.

"I was quite comfortable with the bi-focals before as compared to the progressives you have suggested. I don't see well with them" , new users of products do have issues.

"The new silicon contact lenses I am wearing are thick and my eyes become red", - Adaptation issues are common and helping your customers in this regard is what makes your selling skill perfect.

Empathize and Respond

The immediate way to handle objections is to empathize with the customer and then respond. " Oh! I am sorry to hear that. Can you please give me a bit more detail as to what kind of shops in the market are selling cheap". If the customer challenges you that the same product is available in the market 50% cheap, it is most likely that they are selling counter-feat products.

" Can you please help me to understand how long you have been wearing your new progressives and what sort of issues you are facing" – understanding a bit more of customer's routine and lifestyle can help you to help the customer know more about adapting to progressive lenses.

The same may be the issues in terms of adaptation of silicon hydrogel lenses especially if the patient had been using hydrogel lenses in the past.

Restate and Clarify

Restate the objection and clarify. This will help you to understand the exact problem and the same time builds enormous confidence in customer's mind that you are listening to him and you would definitely take special of him. "

"So you said that the shops in Naif market are selling the same models at 50% cheaper than our price, is that right".

" So you are saying with this small spectacle frame that you are wearing, it is difficult to have clarity with the progressive lenses while you are using the computer, is it so".

"So you mean to say that even after wearing these Silicon Hydrogel lenses for three days, you still don't feel them to as comfortable as the lenses you were wearing in the past?".

Pause and Listen

Developing the habit of Pause and Listen would stand you in good stead while handling objections. Pause and Listen can be practiced all through the sales call.

Your smile, your eye contact, your empathetic 'deep breath', your bent finger on the lips and the nod of the head, all of this body language may indicate to the customer how serious you are in solving the problem and meeting his expectations.

" (Pause) Ma'am, I strongly share your feelings. I can understand how difficult it is for you after having paid so much that your vision is not clear through these lenses. Let me take the measurements again and then I am sure to come out with a solution.". This approach may immediately reduce the tension in the air and bring both parties to an amicable solution.

The more refined you are in this 'Pause and Listen' exercise, the more civilized, cultured and sophisticated sales person you will be.

Reference and Recommendation

Don't try to jump the steps or ignore any part of the objection. This may prove counter-productive. References, testimonials and experiences come handy while solving problems and overcoming objections.

" Mrs.Jane, may I share with you that a customer happened to come to us with the similar problem last week. We suggested to her the same solution and she is quite happy with those lenses now".

The Professional Eye care Practitioner

As the world economy is gradually stabilizing after having been through the crests and troughs of recessionary path, the health care industry in general and optical industry in particular has held ground firmly.

Even in the optical industry, those who have practiced their profession in a dignified way true to the spirit and ethos of their professional integrities, have come out with amazing results.

For the rest, its high time that they do justice to their profession. Its never too late, folks. "People don't buy your products, your company or even You... What they buy is your ability to understand them. Know how to do that and what you'll have is customers for LIFE." - **Michael Oliver**

Objections Sustained

Types of Buyers and Their Objections

Invite to the way of your Lord with wisdom and good advice, and debate with them in the most dignified manner. **Quran : An Nahl :125**

Two shoe salespeople were sent to Africa to open up new markets. Three days after arriving, one salesperson called the office and shared his objections, "I'm returning on the next flight. Can't sell shoes here.

Everybody goes barefoot." At the same time the other salesperson sent an email to the factory, telling "The prospects are unlimited. Nobody wears shoes here!"

In the earlier chapter we had discussed about how different customers have different types of objections and the ways to handle them. In this edition, we will discuss about the different types of prospects vis-a-vis their objections while you present the solutions.

The Combatant

The Combatant as the name suggests is ready with a barrage of his objections in ambush style. The range of issues may cover the product quality, color, specification, delivery time, add-ons, after care, price etc. No sooner you finish solving one objection, he is ready shoot another.

The best way to handle this prospect is to make him seated comfortably first, have him treated well with the niceties of welcome. Build the rapport. Be generous in your smile and relieve him of his stress so that his combat mode can be neutralized.

Jot down the list of objections. At the end of the list you may ensure if he has any more issues to add. Answer those objections in a manner which your prospect understands. Do not jump to the next objection until the previous one has been cleared.

After answering all the objections if the prospect still tries to evade purchase, there is every chance that he is fake prospect who has just come to while away your time.

The Innocent

'Innocence is thought to be charming because it offers delightful opportunities of exploitation' says Mason Cooley. May God bless the Innocent, he is the easiest prospect you would ever have. He speaks what is in his heart and ready to trust your solution without any reservations. Do not take him for a ride to loose him forever. On the contrary, if you help him clear all the doubts and satisfy his needs, he is likely to be your customer for life.

You may share with him the success stories of the product but not be in haste to sell. He gets overwhelmed by your gentleness and annoyed by your pressure.

The Skeptic/Cynic

'It is evident that skepticism, while it makes no actual change in man, always makes him feel better'. Ambrose Bierce

This prospect has an acid tongue. This person walks in with bag full of doubts. He may question the originality of the nose pads or screws to the product itself. He is sarcastic in his approach and dogmatic in his replies.

Show seriousness on your face while attending to his queries. Do not oppose or challenge. Let him blow his trumpet and exhaust his steam. Tell him that he has raised a very important issues and if he would mind elaborating it. This lead to two things. Firstly, that you are giving him importance, secondly he has to re-phrases his objections in such a way it takes the sting out of them. Life is not a bed of roses but a path of thorns. You got bear with these people.

The Reluctant

'Indecision is a virus that can run through an army and destroy its will to win or even to survive', said Wendell Mayes.

This prospect would take a hell of a time to decide. He wanted to start the De-Lay Club and still delaying it. Please do not mistake him. That's how his mental makeup is. Because it look a while for his brain to form while he was in his mother's womb.

If you look at Ned Herrmann's Whole Brain Model, this person is very detail oriented. He needs to study a lot of literature and testimonials before he could decide to purchase the product. He would like keep himself safe from the wrong decisions of life. Does not matter for him to loose millions because of this indecisiveness. Does not matter for him if the whole season goes and new models arrive into the market.

Demonstrate empathy and share with him what his friends or relatives think about the product. Or you may share whatever can gains his trust such as catalogues, warrantee cards etc.

Push him with deadlines and lucrative deals.

" This model is available in very few outlets only in the market".

" This price is valid only for the next 24 hours".

" This is a fast moving model, I cannot guarantee if it will be available tomorrow".

The Genius

This prospect is the Jack of All. He behaves as if he knows everything under the sun. ''Knowing everything means you don't need to think, and that is very dangerous." quotes Garth Nix.

Every time you give an explanation, he will nod his head ' I know, I know' and he would add his genius touch to it. 'This has polarized lenses right. I know about polarized lenses, they polarize light, like north pole and south pole', he will boast. Flatter his ego. That's what makes him comfortable.

" Sir, as you said you are aware about Polarization, may I add that these lenses have nine layers of protection in them'. Start explaining the benefits of each layer such water-proofing, bi-gradient mirror etc.

The Biggies

The Biggy Prospect has a big Ego. They feel that they have to be the center of attention to make their presence felt. These prospects need constant praise like 'The Genius'. They are not keen about discounts. They often would like to buy expensive items.

The most important things for them is to be attended by qualified and experienced sales staff. More often they would like to deal with the branch manager. Be Brief in your explanations. " Madam, anti-reflection reduces the glare enormously and cosmetically will look beautiful on your face". " This is a solid gold frame and we have reserved only few pieces for VIPs like you". Be conservative in words when it comes to Biggies. They get annoyed too often.

Surely, it will work and that is what sales is all about. Dealing with customers accordingly to their mind set.

Customers think and behave differently based on their up-bringing, the environment they live in and their experiences of the past. This is what makes up their personality. Galen, the greek physician, has done well to classify personalities based on body fluids of humans. Ned Herrmann, on the other hand, has come out with his system of thinking preferences based on brain dominance.

Therefore, the wise sales person is the one who develops the art of treating every customer differently based on his or her personality and thinking preferences. It high time you develop this art for your own benefit.

Truth is, I'll never know all there is to know about you just as you will never know all there is to know about me. Humans are by nature too complicated to be understood fully. So, we can choose either to approach our fellow human beings with suspicion or to approach them with an open mind, a dash of optimism and a great deal of candor.

Tom Hanks

The Salesperson's Magic Wand

Presenting Tailor-made Solutions

At the beginning, mankind and the obligation of selfless service were created together. "Through selfless service, you will always be fruitful and find the fulfillment of your desires": this is the promise of the Creator. **Bhagavad Gita 3.10-26**

Once four youth were watching a small calf stuck in the slushy lake bed. They were eager to see how it would manage to get out. As the calf tried to lift one leg, the other three legs went deeper into the mud.

The youths enjoyed the show. Meanwhile a bedouin came that way. He spotted the calf struggling. Immediately he rushed towards the calf and lifted the calf onto his shoulders and walked back to the bank.

The four young men greeted the bedouin and told him that they had been enjoying the drama and he had come and spoilt the fun. They asked him what had made him do this.

The bedouin said, "Brothers, I didn't do it out of pity for the calf. Looking at the calf struggle I felt the pain myself and I felt extremely annoyed; in order to find relief for myself I ran towards the calf and lifted it onto my shoulders."

Empathy is not just feeling like the other person. It is to becoming like him at the moment. It is needless to say this virtue has disappeared among the inhabitants of developed cities, rather thrives among the illiterate bedouins of desert. Ignorance is bliss, you might say.

After identifying the needs of the prospect, invoke the humanity in you. This is the point which makes or breaks your career. This is the essence of a sales call. A well-considered, measured, empathetic solution can make this prospect your life-long disciple. Human instinct is always searching for gurus and mentors with whom we can be associated with till the end. Inter-dependence is the very essence of human society.

Here are the steps to follow to offer solutions :

Re-state the Need :

Restating the need helps you to re-focus on the issue and raises curiosity in customer's mind as to how you are going to help him/her find the solution.

☐ Madam, your prescription shows that you need distance correction as well as near correction. In this case you need a bigger frame for progressive lenses.

☐ Sir, since you said you drive during day time as well at night, you may need anti-reflection coating along with photo-chromatic lenses.

☐ Miss, your astigmatism has increased to -3.00 cyl, that is why you are experiencing severe headache at times.

Offering Solutions :

Usually, sales people spread the range of choices on the table for the customer. The best and the beautiful way to offer sales solutions is to reduce those choices to a few and offer an appropriate solution to the prospect.

This helps the buyer to fall in line with your thinking. This helps the buyer to decide quickly on your offer. If any objections crop up, you can then skillfully deal with them to arrive at a conclusion and close the deal. Please note that the most important thing the customer would like to hear from you is about the benefits the product offers rather than the features. Here are the answers to the above stated needs :

- ➢ Madam, in view of your need for progressive lenses, I am happy to inform you that we have an excellent collection of frames from high end to affordable prices.

- ➢ Let me suggest to you to you this Rayban Rimless Frame with solid gold, which suits your face well. As you know, Rayban is the most renowned brand in the world. I am sure you will feel proud by associating yourself with this brand.

- ➢ This is a hand-crafted piece with a buffalo horn temple which means the quality is exquisite and ever-lasting and adds richness to your profile.

- ➢ The progressives lenses we would like to offer is from Hiko which are made in Germany. Hiko Supreme lenses have been developed with 3D Distort-Free System. Its advanced designed offers aspheric compensation immensely improving clarity and visual comfort with least distortion and high clarity of vision.

- I am happy to offer you Brizal Visi UV coating which is the most advanced anti-reflective lens on the market.
    - Brizal Visi UV coating offers unrivalled performances against the 6 enemies of vision: Glare reduction, smudges, scratches, dust and water and fog.
    - Brizal Visi UV offer your eyes protection against dangerous UV from the front and the back surfaces of the lens ensuring that they offer 10 times more protection from the harmful UV rays.
    - The anti-reflective coating in Brizal lenses means that the glare from oncoming headlights is significantly reduced while driving at night.
    - The Anti-reflective coating on Brizal lenses also means that glare computer screens is reduced, preventing eyes from becoming tired and fatigued throughout the day.
    - This coating transmits 99% transmit light and cosmetically enhance your appearance immensely. Therefore vision and the comfort is unparalleled.

- Miss Reem, I am surprised to see that your astigmatism has increased from -2.00 cyl to -3.00 cyl. It is important that you need to wear your spectacles all the time. However, may I suggest you the Seevell Toric contact lenses with Anti-Gravity Design.
    - The Silicon-Hydrogel material ensures that almost 100% oxygen passes through cornea which prevents you from diseases which arise due to lack of oxygen like in hydrogel lenses.
    - The Anti-Gravity Design ensures that your vision does not blur and fluctuate.

- You can wear these lenses for more than twelve hours and feel the same freshness in the evening as you feel in the morning.

When I discuss about presenting sales solutions with my students, I always use to give them the example of an umbrella. One might buy an umbrella to protect himself from the heat and rain. If the person gets drenched even after holding the umbrella on his head, then what is the purpose of it.

Customers buy products for the benefits they offer. A crow by any other name can look as black. That's the perception a buyer holds. Therefore, always explain the benefits of the products rather than delving too much into the features which serves no purpose. Follow the pattern stated above which, I am sure, will be of help. Be the Guru, there are too many followers around you.

The difference between a sales person and a sales consultant is that the former explains to the customer but the latter enlightens.

Grace and Noble

Closing the Sales

"A customer is the most important visitor on our premises. He is not dependent on us. We are dependent on him. He is not an interruption in

our work. He is the purpose of it. He is not an outsider in our business. He is part of it. We are not doing him a favor by serving him. He is doing us a favor by giving us an opportunity to do so." **Mohandas.K. Gandhi**

Closing the Sales is like writing the last chapter of the book. If you do not feel the warmth after closing it, if you do not feel like reading it again, if you do not feel like recollecting those nice events, jokes, incidences, then there was no point in reading that book.

Closing the sales is similar to that. The customer should feel that he had visited a wonderful shop, met the best sales person in you, asked for your mobile number in good faith, felt proud in buying the product, got all his questions clarified, doubts cleared, objections met and issues solved.

And most importantly shared his happiness with friends and family members so that they too can be part of this eternal bond that you had created.

Follow these steps to close the sales :

Get an ' Yes'

A Direct Close would be ask the customer,

" Shall I proceed with the order of lenses"

" Shall I proceed with printing the invoice"

Alternate Close could be :

" How would you like to pay, Madam.. cash or card?'

A 'hooked' close would be :

"Sir, we have only few pieces of this model left. Shall I book it for you"

An assumptive close would be :

" Ma'am, I will keep this frame aside for you"

What the customer takes home with him along with the product is your smile, your warmth, your hospitality, your care, and soon.

Leave a lasting impression so that you would compel him or her to come back to sooner or later. Thank your customer profoundly for choosing to purchase from you. Do not forget to him or her to say " have your eyes check again in the next six months please , free of charge of course".

Today is here now, so go ahead and jump into it with everything you have. Experience the richness of this day, and you'll carry its unique value with you always.

-- Ralph Marston

Words That Spell Magic

Remember Barney, the magenta colored dinosaur which seized the role of a teacher to inculcate goods habits amongst kids. That is when we all sang and rejoiced along with our children as they learnt their initial lessons on being courteous. The song goes like this :

There are lots of things we can do to be nice,
Sometimes they're hard to remember.
But there are two little things you should never forget,
From January through December.

He's talking 'bout please and thank you, they're called the magic words,
If you want nice things to happen,
They're the words that should be heard,
Remember please and thank you, 'cause they're the magic words.

Elementary as it sounds, but not many are sticklers to this habit. Just recently I saw a post on linkedin.com by someone complaining about lack of manners in one of the restaurants he had visited in London. I was a bit surprised though, since my first lesson on social etiquette was taught to me not by my grandma but by my English teacher, based on the article written by an English man whose name I fail to remember.

Here is a little story on the words of etiquette.

Long time ago a little boy was walking through a park. In the middle of the park there was a tree with a sign on it. The sign said "I am a magic tree. Say the magic words and you will see."

The boy tried to guess the magic words. He tried abracadabra, **supercalifragilisticexpialidocious**, tan-ta-ra, and many more. But none of them worked.

Exhausted, he threw himself on the floor, saying: "Please, dear tree!" and suddenly a big door opened in the trunk. Inside everything was dark, except for a sign which said "Carry on with your magic." Then the boy said "Thank you, dear tree!" With this, the inside of the tree lit up brightly and revealed a pathway leading to a great big pile of toys and chocolate.

The little boy brought all his friends to the magic tree, and they had the best party ever.

Words What We Know And To Learn

This story can be realized in real life too. A mere 'sorry' can cool down tempers. A pleasing gesture towards a driver can you let your car squeeze in between the traffic etc.

As it happened with me last week. A Korean lady had come all the way from Abudhabi to fit her glasses. Apparently she was annoyed that she had been given wrong information by our staff about the place of the service to be rendered. All I had to do is to empathize with her and offer my profound remorse and how I could personally solve her problem. And she lived happily ever after. Hurray!

It is apparent in most showrooms in Gulf to be welcomed by a gorgeously smiling Kabayan, "Good Morning, Sir. Welcome to our store…..".

It also heartening to note that most of the sales staff are well mannered, well-cultured, well-behaved and presentable at least in the major shopping malls. Indeed this has contributed in enhancing the image of Gulf countries as fascinating shopping destinations. Analysts can vouch about the average revenue per person yielded in shopping malls which is substantially better than the street shops. Of course, there are many other factors which contribute to this aspect which is beyond our argument.

Nevertheless, coming back to our discussion about manners and etiquettes, it is needless to say that still a gap is visible that needs to be filled by all of us by improving and improvising our etiquettes which, I am sure, will contribute enormously towards consolidating our relationship with our customers.

First of all, let us mean what we say. And how shall we do that ?

What I mean by that is let your customer feel :

That you are earnest to satisfy him when you say, 'please'.

That you are honestly remorseful when you say, 'sorry'.

That you are greatly indebted and appreciative when you say ' thank you'.

How do we do that... is by using our gestures or in any manner that you can convey your feelings.

Supposing if a customer walks in and asks for a rimless frame. Rather than pointing it towards the shelf next to the clinic, please lead the customer yourself towards the shelf with your kind request 'please follow me Ma'am'. If you are an expert enough, suggest the best spectacle frame adding ' I hope this will fit you perfectly'.

More often than not, you will find your customer accepting your choice. On the contrary, I have noticed on quite a few occasions where the sale staff had pointed to the customer to go behind the wall or next to the cashier or in the drawer underneath wooden shelf and check it for himself. Shame!

Learning The Local Language

Survival of a sales person with lack of understanding of the local language and culture can only be a miracle. There are a few dozen words in Arabic which could help you to cast your magic spell by learning them.

Customers are quite comfortable dealing with people in the language they speak, especially in their mother tongue.

When Abu Aiman was very annoyed with the delay of his german made lenses with blue filters in 1.74 index, Waleed could calm him down instantly by expressing,

"ehna waayid aasifeen lil iza'aj, Abu Aiman.

Wasalat Adasaathak. Al hain fil jamaarak. Bus thetaaj intazar yomain. Aasifeen liththakheer

(we are extremely sorry for the inconvenience Abu Aiman. Your lenses came. Now they are in customs. Just need a couple of days. Sorry for the delay).

The following expressions may perhaps help

Faddalee Madam, Kaif yumkinanee musadathich (Welcome Madam, how may I help you)

Istharee Madam (Please have a seat, Madam)

Dactoor mashgool al hain (Doctor is busy now)

Aasif li' ibgaayik thantazir, Sayyadhy. (Sorry for keeping you waiting, Sir)

shoofakum khareeban (See you soon)

And there are plenty to learn.

Simple effort from your side to learn the language can yield an enormous benefit to the relationship with your customers. All the best. A'thamanna lak nahaar sayeed.

If you talk to a man in a language he understands, that goes to his head. If you talk to him in his language, that goes to his heart.
Nelson Mandela

Advance Selling Techniques Through NLP

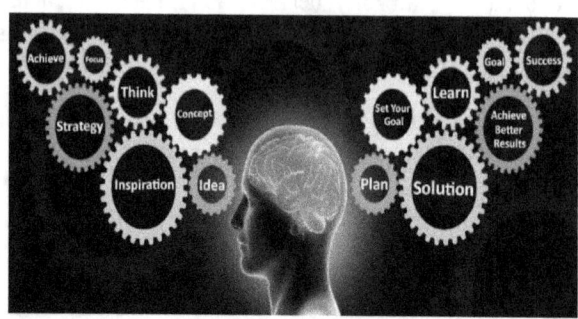

It's about four years since I started to write in Eyezone. " *The bad news is **time flies**. The good news is **you** are the **pilot**'*, said a post on Pinterest which I obediently admit.

We are all pilots in our own right. Everyone of us is responsible for the passengers whom we carry on-board. " Everyone of you is a shepherd and responsible for his flock", says Prophet Muhammad. Therefore I dedicate this article to those wonderful Pilots, Shepherds, Masters and Leaders who have keenly and avidly read my articles, texted me their feedback, recognized me when we met, encouraged me for my enthusiasm and criticized me for my flaws. Undoubtedly it has been a wonderful journey travelling through the history along with you riding on the crests and troughs of time.

Now, we shall climb up the tree of knowledge to pluck the divine fruit to satiate our hunger; to know more and do more.

Dear readers, I now take this opportunity to introduce to you, NLP, that is Neuro Linguistic Programming.

Neuro Linguistic Programming

What is NLP and how is it going to help us in sales or in our personal lives. In the pursuit of knowing this subject, I would gratefully borrow some content from Joseph O'Connor's book, NLP Workbook and adapt my learnings to our field, optics.

There are many explanations of NLP, *each like beam of light shining from a different angle, picking out the whole shape and shadow of the subject.*

NLP evolved after a great amount of studying human communication by applying various tools in various fields such as sports, business, sales, law and education. The name 'Neuro-Linguistic Programming' comes from the three areas it brings together :

N   - Neurology – The mind and how humans think

L   - Linguistics – The use of language and it affects us

P   - Programming – How we sequence our actions to achieve our goals

A boy asked his mother, " Ma, what is NLP?"

His mother replied, " I will tell you in a moment, Son. But first you have to do something so that you can understand. See there, you grandfather over chair. Go and ask him how his arthritis is today."

The boy went to his grandfather and asked, " Nanu, how is your arthritis today"

' Oh, a bit bad son,' replied the old man. 'It's always worse in damp weather. I can hardly move my fingers today.' A look of pain crossed his face.

The boy went back to his mother. 'He said it is bad. It is bad. I think it hurts him. Are you going to tell me what NLP is now ?'

'In a minute, I promise,' replied his mother. 'Now go over and ask your granddad what was the funniest thing that you did when you were very young.'

The old man's face lit up. 'Oh,' he smiled, 'there was the time when you and your friend played Father Christmas and sprinkled talcum power all over the bathroom pretending it was snow. I laughed but I didn't have to clean it up.' He stared into the distance with a smile.

' Then there was the time I took you out for a walk. You were singing a nursery rhyme loudly. A man went past and gave you a nasty look. He thought you were noisy and asked me to tell you to be quiet. You turn around and said to him, 'If you don't like me singing, you can go and boil your head.' The old man chuckled.

The boy went back to his mother, ' did you hear what Nanu said', he asked.

'Yes', his mother replied. 'You changed how he felt in few words. That's NLP.'

Basic Principles of NLP

NLP has 6 basic principles known as the pillars of NLP.

1. You
2. The Presuppositions
3. Rapport
4. Outcome
5. Feedback
6. Flexibility

We will delve more into the aforesaid points in the next issue. However, while applying these principles in our sales life, most sales people are cautiously optimistic that its principles are worthy of utilization.

Stephen Covey's 2nd habit of "begin with the end in mind" applies, a clear vision of a path to a successful sale, looking for visual clues that monitor how successful your sales pitch is, or whether your attempts at conversation are working well or failing miserably.

Neuro-linguistic principles help us to be flexible in our approach by keenly looking for cues from customers to overcome objections and win the hearts, minds, and wallets of potential clients. To get desired results, staff members must have an inherent drive to succeed that allows them to vary their presentation wherever necessary.

Proponents of neuro-linguistic ideology present NLP as a unique opportunity to monitor the flow of conversation and engage prospects with a logical, sensible sales pitch.
Worthy sales professionals retain the ability to distance themselves from failure and personal rejection as critical to establishing a distinction between a person and their behavior.

On the whole, NLP is still a developing science which is worth considering in our sales pitch with our customers on a day to day basis. We will explore it thoroughly going forward. Until then enjoy your summer holidays.

"One ought, every day at least, to hear a little song, read a good poem, see a fine picture, and, if it were possible, to speak a few reasonable words." **Johann Wolfgang von Goethe,**

Self Improvement In The Light of NLP

An old man sat outside the walls of a great city. When travelers approached, they would ask the old man, "What kind of people live in this city?" The old man would answer, "What kind of people live in the place where you came from?" If the travelers answered, "Only bad people live in the place where we came from," the old man would reply, "Continue on; you will find only bad people here."

But if the travelers answered, "Good people live in the place where we came from," then the old man would say, "Enter, for here too, you will find only good people."

Color of this world is based on the color of your eyes, color of your glasses. The way you perceive the things; your understanding, your thoughts and your experiences. Good and Bad people you will find everywhere in the world, in every country, in every society it is up to us, what we are looking for.

Its All About You

In Neuro Linguistic Programming, the first basic principle is 'You'. Its all about you and your development. Your emotional state and the attitude you develop towards your life. The knowledge and skills you acquire through the process of learning and utilizing NLP. Like a painter either you be content painting your bathroom wall or you can endeavor to paint your living room the Starry Nights of Van Gogh.

You need to have congruence between your thoughts, speech and actions. In clear words, 'Walk the Talk and Talk the Walk', as Joseph Connor says.
How may you do that ?
All you have to do is to pick up a piece of paper and pen and write down what you need to do with your life. In self-help parlance it is called Goal Setting.

How To Set Your Goals

Most self-help books talk about SMART goals. We are taught the acrostic of SMART goals as follows :

S -> Specific

M -> Measurable

A -> Achievable

R -> Realistic

T -> Time Bound

The NLP model enables us to go beyond mere "goal setting" into the actual "programming" of our minds to drive us towards our desired goal. And how ?

The NLP goal setting model addresses this by getting goals sensory specific which means utilizing our five senses. But it doesn't stop there. For, the brain not only uses the sensory system, it also uses our word meanings that drive the sensory system. For this reason, the NLP Goal Setting Model makes absolutely sure that we program ourselves in such a way as to drive our very neurology and physiology towards obtaining our desired goal. This is sometimes called as **The Well-Formed Outcome Model.**

Following points enable you to effectively identify your desired state and move towards future:

State the goal in positive terms.

Describe the Present Situation and compare it with the desired future goal.

- Where are you now? (For Eg : Sales Staff)
- Where do you want to be? (For Eg : Branch Manager)
- What do you want to get there? (For Eg : Knowledge and Skill)

Specify the goal in Sensory Based Terms.

- What will you see, hear, feel, etc., when you have it? (*I will see people following my command, I will feel responsibility, I will hear appreciation for my efforts*)
- What steps or stages are involved in reaching this goal? (*Acquiring knowledge and skill, managerial training, showing results during probation*)
- Engage all of your senses in this description process to employ more of your brain and nervous system.
- Have you broken down your goal into small enough chunks so that each is do-able?

Specify the goal in a way that you find compelling.

Is the goal compelling? Visualize this goal as if you have achieved it.

Self-initiated and maintained.

Is the goal something that you can initiate yourself and maintain?

Your goal must be something that you can initiate and maintain. It must not be something dependent on other people. Make sure that your goal reflects things that you can directly affect.

State the Context of the goal.

Where, when, how, with whom, etc. will you get this goal?

Test your goal by applying it to a context: when, where, with who, etc. to make sure that it is going to be fitting and appropriate. Re-adjust your goal to make sure that it fits. (*For example, I would like become the branch manager of XX branch which I am sure to increase their sagging sales by 20% by focusing on adding new customers to our business*)

State the Resources needed to achieve the goal.

- What resources will you need in order to get this goal?
- Who will you have to become?
- Who else has achieved this goal?
- Have you ever had or done this before?
- What prevents you from moving toward it and attaining it now?

Evidence Procedure.

- How will you know that your goal has been realized?
- What will let you know that you have attained that desired state?

NLP provides us with a process that will ensure all of these points are covered, that your goals are SMART and that your unconscious mind and energy is aligned in achieving it. The **NLP** process involves understanding you put your memories in respective pigeon holes. The **NLP** process ties our sensory perceptions to our goal as we go through its stages.

As it is known, ninety five percent of the people in the world do not set goals for themselves. Only five percent do. It is apparent to you now, whom the ninety five percent follow. So what's the recourse for you. Look at the goal post and go for the kick. Goaaaal!!!!

A dream written down with a date becomes a Goal. A goal broken down into steps becomes a Plan. A plan backed by actions makes your dream come true. **Greg Reid**

Developing Your Communication Skills
The NLP Method

I don't know for sure who expressed it, but time and again have experienced the below statement to be so true.

" 10% of conflict is due to difference in opinion, 90% is due to delivery and tone of voice".

Here we go to see an example which you may take liberty to laugh but deserves serious pondering.

CEO to Manager
Today at 11 '0 clock, there will be a total eclipse of the sun. This is when the sun disappears behind the moon for two minutes. As this something that cannot be seen everyday, time will be allowed for the employees to view the eclipse in the parking lot. Staff should meet in the lot at 10 to 11 when I will be delivering a short speech introducing the eclipse and giving some background information. Safety goggles will be made available at a small cost

Manager to Department Head
Today , at ten to eleven, all staff should meet at the car park. This will be followed by a total eclipse of the sun which will appear for two minutes. For a moderate cost this will made safe with goggles. The CEO will deliver a short speech to give us all some information. This is not something that can be seen everyday.

Department Head to Floor Manager
The CEO will give a short speech to make the sun disappear for two minutes in the form of an eclipse. This is something that cannot be seen everyday so staff will meet at the car park at ten or eleven. This will be safe if you pay a moderate cost.

Floor Manager to Supervisor
Ten or eleven staff are to go to the car park where the CEO will eclipse the sun for two minutes. This does not happen everyday. It will be safe and as usual it will cost you.

Supervisor to Staff
Some staff will go to the car parking to see the CEO disappear. It is a pity it does not happen everyday.

The NLP Communication Model

The NLP Communication Model, developed by Tad James & Wyatt Woodsmall (1988) from the work of Richard Bandler & John Grinder (1975), is one of the key structures in NLP.

As humans we know and admit that we are being bombarded with plethora of information. Our five senses are constantly taking in information and processing it at an average rate of 4 million bits per second. In other words, not all information is absorbed into our mind. We tend to Delete, Distort and Generalize information which passes through the unique filters in our brain.

After the information is subjected to the due process, impulses consolidate and evolve into what we call as 'Thought'. Thereafter, these thoughts conjoin to form Internal Representations. Like if someone shows a stone face towards the magician banishing the elephant into thin air or the street kids cacophony in tying the tail of the dragon fly, or the old man snapping at his wife's bickering are all instantaneous triggers which motivate a person's behaviors.

Our thoughts, feelings and behaviors stem from our unique filters. These filters vary from deeply unconscious processes to more conscious processes, namely:

Meta Programs - Unconscious filters which form the 'blueprint' of every individual. The reason why different people behave differently.

Values - Lasting beliefs of individuals differentiating between what is right and wrong.

Beliefs - State of person's faith based on which values are formed.

Attitudes – Our behavior based on towards specific things based on Beliefs and values we have.

Memories – Past individual and collective experiences.

Past Decisions – These are the past decisions about who we are and what we are capable of.

The Information Shrink In Our Mind

What happens to the loads of information that reaches our mind. Apparently, our mind becomes choosy as to what is needed and what is not. Through a number of filters, the information is shrunk to 134 bits that our conscious mind can cope with. The filters do this by :

Deletion - to attempt to actively pay attention we focus on what seems most important at any one particular moment in time and allow the rest to pass us by.

The most common example I would cite is using mobile phones while driving. That is, when we try to concentrate on two things at a time, most important things may also get deleted. In other words, concentration on the road may become less priority and hence we end up with bad accidents.

Distortion - occurs when we make shifts in our experience of sensory data by making misrepresentations of reality. For example, when we plan something we use distortion to construct appealing imaginary futures. The aforesaid example of the CEO vanishing into thin air can be one.

Generalization - is the process by which we draw global conclusions based on one, two or more experiences.

Have you heard people saying that there is no more peace in the world just because in one corner of the world there is war. Or people belonging to a particular race or tribe are bad because some one you had met was bad. Every time I cross the road I run fearing for my life, because I had been hit once as a child.

Generalizations are mechanisms which generate beliefs and they may be useful or dangerous depending upon how we approach.

How Does NLP Communication Apply to Optics

Whether in optical sales or dealing with customers in any field, it is vital to understand the beliefs customers adhere to and the values they stand for.

For example in Gulf, many men would not prefer a golden color frame rather would opt for silver. This is because gold is prohibited in their religion. Their adherence to their belief can be so stringent that they would not prefer even a gold plated frame. So the solution is to present eyewear of any hue other than gold.

Women would not prefer to deal with men. I have noticed this attitude among women belonging to various nationalities and religion who would rather be happy to meet a lady doctor or salesperson than a man. So what do we do. Let the lady in the showroom lead from the front.

Bad memories lead to bad mouth. Especially when customers in Gulf are so habitually expressive when they are faced with bad experience. All of your ten years of relationship with your customer will go down the drain if today was your bad day to make your customer unhappy. So the solution is, bend your back to make your customer happy or bend forward to apologize. Chill! Its winter folks.

The biggest communication problem is we do not listen to understand. We listen to reply. **Anonymous**

Building Rapport With Your Customers
The NLP Dimension

Once upon a time two brothers who lived on adjoining farms fell into conflict. It was the first serious rift in 40 years of farming side by side.

Then the long collaboration fell apart. It began with a small misunderstanding and it grew into a major difference, and finally it exploded into an exchange of bitter words followed by weeks of silence.

One morning there was a knock on John's door. He opened it to find a man with a carpenter's toolbox. "I'm looking for some work. Could I help you in anyway ?" he asked.

"Yes," said the older brother. "I do have a job for you. Look across the creek at that farm.

That's my neighbor, in fact, it's my younger brother. Last week there was a meadow between us and he took his bulldozer to the river to dig and now there is a creek between us. Well, he doesn't who I am. See that pile of lumber lying there? I want you to build me a fence – an 8-foot fence – so I won't need to see his place anymore. Sounds good ?"

The carpenter said, "I think I understand the situation. Get me the required material and I'll be able to do a job that pleases you."

The older brother arranged for the supplies and then he was off for the day.

The carpenter worked hard all that day measuring, sawing, nailing.

About sunset when the farmer returned, the carpenter had just finished his job. The farmer's eyes opened wide, his jaw dropped.

There was no fence there at all. It was a bridge… a bridge stretching from one side of the creek to the other! A fine piece of work handrails and all – and the neighbor, his younger brother, was coming across, his <u>hand outstretched</u>.

"You are quite a fellow to build this bridge after all I've said and done."

The two brothers stood at each end of the bridge, and then they met in the middle, taking each other's hand. They turned to see the carpenter hoist his toolbox on his shoulder. "No, wait! Stay a few days. I've a lot of other projects for you," said the older brother.

"I'd love to stay on," the carpenter said, "but, I have many more bridges to build.

Rapport – The NLP Perspective

Rapport is the quality of relationship that results in mutual trust and responsiveness. In fact, it is the first foundation of trust building. Rapport is about empathizing, that is understanding and respecting the way how another person sees the world. All activities such as a looking into the eyes of customers with all keenness and care, nodding our head, our tone and our responsive facial expressions, all kinds of mirroring generates respect within the mind of the customer and thus rapport is built, brick by brick. Rapport cannot be built instantly. Its takes its own course of time depending upon the subject and evolves into trust.

Seven Levels of Rapport

Remember this thumb rule, " People like people who are like themselves"

ENVIRONMENT - The way you present yourself

Most companies in this region as well as around the world insist on their sales staff wearing uniform to reflect their organization culture. But keeping the uniform neat, well-ironed, fresh and smelling perfectly depends on the individual. Likewise a fresh smiling face is more appealing than a tired sweaty one. This creates an environment to indulge in and engage with each other in a cordial manner.

BEHAVIOUR – The way you behave with your customers

The very objective of selling a product to a customer to effect a behavioral change in him. While we discuss NLP, Programming is designed to use mutual behaviors to achieve the intended goals.

Matching behavior is not only about building relationships, it is about behaving in a way that the other person is most likely to understand.

CAPABILITIES– The skills you represent

Birds of same feather flock together. People enjoy the company of those with whom they share the same interests. The talents you have and recognize in others stem from what is important to you and your customer. When you try to understand the issues of the customer and match them with your capabilities to resolve those issues, synergy evolves and thus builds rapport.

VALUES – The values you exhibit

Your values represent what is important to you. They determine how you behave, what skills you draw on, what decisions you make and how you present yourself. You customer may gets attracted to you perhaps you share the same values like him. Commonly held values are typically what holds a team together and what gives a sense of purpose to the styles of your business.

BELIEFS – The beliefs you reflect

Shared beliefs hold cultures, communities, organizations, and teams together. Your beliefs show in everything you do. So does this apply to your customers as well. Beliefs are not facts; they are emotionally held opinions that will mostly have been formed early in your life. You customer may find himself drawn to you or the product you sell without knowing consciously why, only to discover later that deep down they hold the same beliefs as him.

IDENTITY – The kind of person you are.

We are drawn to people like ourselves, in type, in style, in interests, in behavior, in appearance, in beliefs, which all adds up to the kind of people we are. Entrepreneurs rate other entrepreneurs. Sport people value other sports people. Musicians spend time with musicians. Engineers value engineers. We are by our very nature, tribal.

MISSION – Your purpose in life.

Customers get attracted to you because you share their purpose. They feel and start to believe that your purpose goes beyond your own self. That you are more concerned with what you want to give to others and solve their problems of life.

Achieving what you want in a way that enables or supports others to achieve what they want is at the heart of win-win deal.

Speak in such a way that others love to *listen* to you.
Listen in such a way that others love to *speak* to you.
Anonymous

Special offer !_Optimism @ 100% Discount

Did you think I too will spend my days in search of food,

Tell petty stories, worry myself with thoughts,

Hurt others by my acts, turn senile with grey hair

And end up as fodder to the relentless march of time

As yet another faceless man?

Poem by Subramania Bharathi

There is a story of identical twins. One was a hope-filled optimist. "Everything is coming up roses!" he would say. The other twin was a sad and hopeless pessimist. The worried parents of the boys brought them to the local psychologist.

He suggested to the parents a plan to balance the twins' personalities. "On their next birthday, put them in separate rooms to open their gifts. Give the pessimist the best toys you can afford, and give the optimist a box of manure." The parents followed these instructions and carefully observed the results.

When they peeked in on the pessimist, they heard him audibly complaining, *"I don't like the color of this computer . . I'll bet this* **calculator will break . . . I don't like the game . . . I know someone who's got a bigger toy car than this . . ."*

Tiptoeing across the corridor, the parents peeked in and saw their little optimist gleefully throwing the manure up in the air. He was giggling. *"You can't fool me! Where there's this much manure, there's got to be a pony to play with!"*

Global Negativity

Let's visualize this scenario. You wake up in the morning and there stretches your hand searching for your mobile phone. You slide your screen to check your Whatsapp messages only to glue at the videos of rain causing havoc in some parts of Gulf or a big building reduced to ashes on the countryside. "OMG! Can't believe this", you groan. Switch on the TV and you get bombs blasting the airports, or some plane crash. Gosh! This is insane, you shout.

A deluge of negative news bombarding us from all sides. Neighbor lost his job, office air-conditioner stops working, petrol prices gone up, school bus carrying children met with accident, shipment did not reach in time, boss was nasty, chronic constipation et al.

Someone rightly said, " Negativity perpetuates itself, breeds dissatisfaction and clutters the mind. And when the mind is cluttered with negativity, happiness is harder to come by."

Scenario At Retail Front

Now let's look at the retail front. Every business has its own bell curve. The cyclical demand and sluggishness. Like we see in Gulf during the beginning of the year, vacation time peaks, seasonal holiday business, festival time rush etc. Business during these times is massive which helps the sales staff reach their targets and puts a canine to canine smile on their faces. You can feel the freshness in the air, radiant faces, positive synergy among staff, team spirit etc.

The same is not the case during off seasons. Shoppers struggle to sell. Customers' either ask for less expensive products or bargain for more discounts. Sales turnover gets affected. Probably, fifty percent down or even more. Mood in the market becomes subdued. Owners must have lose their sleep. Salaries get delayed, leave pay hike aside. Overall, pessimism prevails, permeates and personifies into pale faces.

How Shall We Overcome Pessimism

The above heading can also be re-written as "How shall we enhance our optimism". Its that simple. Mere change of words.

What is happening to you or people around you is not new. It has happened in the past and it likely to happen in the future. Like Isaac Newton said, " What goes up must come down." That is the gravity of life and so does it apply to your business too.

All things are here to pass. The great pharaohs have passed, Hitler and Mussolini have passed, the world wars have passed, the great depression and recession of 1930s and 2008s has passed. And we are all alive and kicking. Alhumdullilah.. Alleluia... Let's pray praise the Great God for all the bounties he has showered on us. Strong hands, strong legs, a thinking mind and a captivating face. We have it all. Let's summon up courage and gather pace. " A Disbeliever is the one who gets lost into horizon. A Believer is the one who looks for the horizon in what has been lost", said Allama Iqbal, the poet, thinker and philosopher of the sub-continent.

Here are the steps to follow :

1. Believe in the purpose of your life

(Eg. that you are here to support people to get a healthy living)
2. Believe that you are the one who is going to lead from the front to make it happen
3. Focus on the possibilities, not the impossibilities (Eg. Target every customers to upsell or change for something better)
4. Don't go it alone. Team up with your colleagues.
5. Find new ways to improve yourself and pursue your cause. (Eg. Like improving your communication, upgrading yourself with the latest technique etc)
6. Spirituality is good. It gives you emotional comfort. (A prayer or two before going to sleep, or giving charity helps)
7. Get rid of negative thoughts, words or action. (Eg. If someone asks you "how's the business?", you may reply " definitely good under the present circumstances", rather than faking your smile and saying " Wallah! Taa'baan)
8. Be inquisitive of new ideas and implement them. (Not just the same old 'Buy Two Get 1 Free')

To sum it up, all it needs is to shift the gear. See the better side of life. Be grateful for what we have and learn how to utilize the existing resources. If ever you know Hellen Keller who was deaf, blind and complete lack of language. If she could make it to the Alabama Women's Hall of Fame, you can make it far better.

Its about time to go for the positive change. Want to toss the coin to know the result? Go ahead, but do it like Jai did in the hindi film "Sholay". He had 'Heads' on both sides of the coin.

Sales people with optimistic expectations sold more than 37% than those whose were pessimistic.

Metlife Case Study

Things We Should Abstain From while in Sales

But examine everything carefully; hold fast to that which is good; abstain from every form of evil. **Thessalonians :21-22**

I am writing this piece on the first day of Ramadan, a month which is meant for self-abstinence and self-reform. Simply put how I can become a better person than I used to be.

In this context, let me narrate this story to you.

A boy 'n a girl were playing together. The boy had a collection of marbles. The girl had some sweets with her. The boy told the girl that he will give her all his marbles in exchange for her sweets. The girl agreed. The boy kept the biggest 'n the most beautiful marble aside 'n gave the rest to the girl. The girl gave him all her sweets as she had promised. That night, the girl slept peacefully. But the boy couldn't sleep as he kept wondering if the girl had hidden some sweets from him the way he had hidden his best marble.

If you don't give your hundred percent in what you are doing, you'll always keep doubting others and keep blaming them.

In the view of this subject, I had been in discussion with many owners and managers about the staff attitude and behavior and what steps do we need take to correct it.

Some of the points mentioned below needs our serious attention while making our showrooms a better place to work in.

- Cleanliness
- Tidiness
- Aroma
- Quarrelling
- Distraction from Mobile
- Attending another customer
- Appearance

Abstain from dirt

It is apparent that brand awareness is high in Gulf region and hence we all abundantly sell branded products Viz. Chanel, Tiffany and Co, Versace, Prada, Miu Miu, Dior, Gucci and what not. This means to say that 'you' represent these brands to your customers and hence you have live up to their expectations. Whilst displaying these brands on the shelf, if you give the customer even an iota of a reason to assume that store cleanliness is not a priority, the customer spends no time to leave your store and buy the same merchandize from elsewhere.

Therefore, first impressions count. In Gulf, as we know, dirt is pervasive all around because we are surrounded by sand. It but natural to see a thin layer of dust prevailing on the shelf though you might have cleaned it ten times during the day. Hence, ' *make it glitter'* is a thumb rule.

Abstain from disorderliness

Along with cleanliness comes orderliness as well i.e. to keep the right things at the right place. Tatty posters, crumbled brochures, torn blow ups, broken banners, scattered catalogues have no place in a showroom. Keeping your store tidy should be a routine on your check-list of things to do.

Abstain from bad odor

Does your store smell clean and fresh? Sometimes we become immune or used to the smell of our store. In this case, you can ask your friends or new employees to give their opinion.

The same applies to our body odor as well. Most employees work 8 to 9 hours a day at a stretch. It is but natural to lose your freshness during the day. A pleasant perfume for the body and few bits of mint to freshen the mouth will do good especially when you are smoker, the worst habit one can ever have.

Abstain from quarrelling

It might be unusual but it does happen. Some customers lose their temper and indulge in quarrelling. Follow the simple steps as below:

- Remain calm. When a customer starts being rude, there is nothing to be gained by responding in a similar manner.
- Don't take it personally.
- Use your best listening skills.
- Actively sympathize.
- Apologize gracefully.
- Find a solution. If not,
- Seek help from your superior.

Abstain from attending mobiles

If you are in a serious discussion with you customer to sell the latest technology in the progressive lenses and suddenly your boss calls you.

What do you do ? Answering mobiles or telephone while in discussion causes frustration in the other person. While you are in a sales call, it is best not to attend telephones or in the case of an emergency hand it over to you colleague.

Most telephone operators have an automated mail box where the caller can leave the message.

Abstain from dealing with another customer

Most sale persons tend to get excited when another customer walks in while they are dealing with the existing customer. Therefore, they tend to disrupt the present conversation in order to shake a hand or say few words of greetings to please the other one.

Generally, I have noticed this infuriates the present customer who walks out in a huff or at least shows frustration. If at all, there is a situation that you would have to attend the second customer, you better seek permission from the first one and apologize to him when you return to him.

Abstain from untidy appearance

There are three rules that all sales people should use when deciding what they should look like to customers. If you do it right, people will start liking you without knowing really why.

Be Clean. Never be dirty in any way. Dirt disgusts and spurns customers. Therefore, clean body with clean clothes are mandatory.

Dress Smart. In optical showrooms, it is best to wear formal attire. A suit or a blaze will definitely add value to your attire. Abstain from wearing crumbled cloths..

Look Sharp. Have a decent haircut. Trim your moustache. Abstain from unshaven rugged face. Ladies can pin-up their hair-do.

Ramadan is known for big shopping days. Let's hope that you will mend your ways by following the above and make the best out this month. Ramadan Kareem.

Learn from yesterday, live for today, hope for tomorrow. The important thing is not to stop questioning. **Albert Einstein**

Port Folio Management

" O mankind, indeed We have created you from male and female and made you peoples and tribes that you may know one another" **Al Quran – Surat Hujuraat**.

What is Port Folio Management ?

Let's answer what is a Port Folio first. In 1722, the word Port came from Porto meaning 'carrying' and Folio meaning 'loose sheet of papers' , in essence ' carrying a collection of loose sheets of paper'. Later on as years passed by we came to understand that it is a 'collection of ' something or other mostly an investment tool.

Port Folio Management in optical retail can be defined as "**The art and science of selecting, dispensing and managing the right optical** products for the showroom in terms of minimum risk and maximum return of profitability.

In most companies in Gulf, the showroom manager has a limited choice in product selection as it mostly decided by the top management. What products need to be purchased and stocked in showroom is at the complete discretion of the owners. However, within the product mix, the showroom manager can always use his preference to pick particular models, colors and size as per the demand and sale-ability of the products.

Ideal Port Folio for Optical Retail

Have you ever heard about the quintessential Pheriwala of the indian street. Most of us consider him to be a smart Port Folio Manager. He usually carries a small round cane-basket on head which is stuffed with every known product produced on earth. From different shapes of combs to different sizes of needles. Soaps, jugs, hanker-chiefs, spoons, frying pans, you name it, he has it. Ask him for a cheap electric shaver, he would sell you an expensive one. Even though, he does carry a couple of the cheap ones made in the cottages of Delhi.

Port Folio management is also a very popular strategy in stock markets to manage your investments. That is to have a list of very selective stocks in your kitty which yield better returns over a period of time.

In "Optical" Sense, Portfolio Management in optical showroom relates to the optical products which can be categorized as Sunglasses, Spectacle Frames, Contact Lenses, Solutions and Accessories. An ideal percentage of business could be 30% Sunglasses, 40% Spectacle Frames, 25% Contact Lenses and 5% rest. This means more than 65% of your business is depending on prescriptions.

Steps towards Port Folio Management

As a first step, analyze and let yourself know if your business is matching up to the aforesaid percentage. It is not a happy situation to see if your showroom is selling more sunglasses except by as a strategy. What I mean to say is, I am often prone to hear from the showroom managers especially in shopping malls that 75% of their total business is from Sunglasses. That means, the guys in the showroom are not doing enough to build their business based on the vision care requirement of their customers rather than selling Sunglasses as a fashion accessories.

In contrast, if that had been done willfully by explaining the harmful effects of Ultra Violet Radiation to the patients and let every walk-in customer get educated at your hands and walk out with a pair of sunglasses, thanking heavens for getting a chance to meet you, trust me, you are one of a kind in this optical world.

Having said the above, an analysis of your portfolio will certainly enlighten you to which way you should move forward. And the best way, I said, it to tilt your business towards more prescriptions related sales which, I am sure, will reward you with more customer satisfaction and increase in loyalty. Once you have gained customers' trust, you can then introduce to them different options in vision care, which we will discuss at length later.

If you would agree to my point, it is but natural that you will, now plan in accordance with our agreement and set forth things in the right direction. That is, to acquire sufficient and knowledge and information related products that can be prescribed, develop your staff's skill so as to efficiently communicate your knowledge to your customers and execute what you had planned by monitoring the sales figures regularly.

Then your Portfolio management will look like " ***the art and science of making decisions about investment mix, matching investments to objectives, and balancing risk against performance***" rather than the loose sheet of papers we see in most optical shops which immediately reflects your business acumen.

Try and practice it. I am sure you will be amazed by the outcome.

Most of the important things in the world have been accomplished by people who have kept on trying when there seemed to be no hope at all. **Dale Carnegie**

Relationship Dynamics With Colleagues

Workforce in Gulf is heterogeneous, predominantly of mixed nationalities, we know. Mostly Levantine Arabs and South Asians occupy the front line in retail stores. Ostensibly a rainbow of nationalities, cultures, languages and belief systems lead to civilizational acquaintances as much as inter-cultural skirmishes.

Peak season has its own complexities. As the volume of business increases so does the work load resulting in a stressful environment within the stores as well as at the back end, with warehouse staff of the company or suppliers whom you deal with.

Everybody is out to meet their individual targets and win the treasure bag of incentives and commissions. Shortcomings faced during the peak season such as orders not arriving in time so that they can be delivered in time, misplacing items meant for the customer, spectacles not being fitted in accordance with the specifications, receiving wrong powers as against the orders placed, lack of adequate staff to handle the rush, an indifferent Branch Manager who aggravates the situation rather than solving it; all these can be nerve wracking and subject your temperament to test. These are some of the numerous issues that have a direct impact on the relationship with your colleagues in your organization.

Lean season issues are different altogether. Morale of the staff will be down apparently in conjunction with drop in sales. In a Buyer's market, staff have to over work to meet their targets. Discounts offered to the customers will be more, hence profits will be down. Truncated targets will look like kilimanjaro's peak to climb. In a sluggish day, any missed sales opportunity will have an emotional impact on sales-staff leading to frustration and in-store rivalry to outdo each other.

Any lapse in terms of delayed supply, wrong prescription, a particular model or color being out-of-stock, computer network issues, warehouse answering the phone, all trivial issues can have a devastating effect on the tempo and hence can lead to inter-colleague misdemeanor and a politically charged atmosphere.

How To Maintain Relationships And Avoid Politics

The above situations are a part and parcel of your professional life. It might change its form and size, but just cannot be avoided. Therefore, while encountering such situations, the following steps can help :

1.Rapport Is Important

Rapport moves mountains. Many a times we have observed this in various facets of life; in different departments of government, in schools, in hospitals, in trains etc. In getting the trade license issued in a day, in a getting a preferred seat for your child in school, fixing an appointment with the renowned cardiac specialist, or just a captivating smile by the lady to get a seat in the moving train, rapport has always helped. Therefore, it needless to say that a strong rapport with your colleagues is a foundational requirement for the growth of business in your store. As some one rightly said, " *Rapport is like standing on wet cement. The longer you stand, the more difficult is to leave. And even if you leave, you leave your footprints on it."*

2. Be Supportive - Always

Humans are bound to form impressions and opinions about other all the time. It takes one-tenth of a second to form an impression about somebody in the first encounter.

To this extent, we need to learn a bit about Impression Management, a conscious or subconscious process in which people attempt to influence the perceptions of self or other people.

To be known as a helpful, accessible, approachable and amiable person can offset any negative thoughts that may arise because of your thoughtless, spontaneous action.

Professional jealousy is a common tendency in most organizations. Most professional relationships are based on your usefulness and overall goodwill.

3. Trustworthiness

If you have problems with your colleagues or seniors, it is best to keep it with you itself rather than drum beat around wherever you go. This creates a very bad impression about you within the organization. If at all you feel to vent your anger, choose the right moment and express your concerns in a delicate and professional way rather than being abusive or using an unpleasant language.

In the same way, if your colleagues have confided any issues with you, it is at best to stay with you like a guarded secret. Once people come to know that you have spoken about anything they have discussed with you, you will lose the trust and respect in their eyes.

4. Gossiping

'Talking badly about someone else while aren't there to defend themselves says more about than the person you are talking about', says a quote.

Gossips are destructive and sometimes lethal. But the fact is that it always exists along with the air we breathe, no matter what you do. Gossip can be positive if you appreciate a person behind his back which will always generate positive energy with in the team.

Nevertheless, Bad Gossip is disintegrative in nature. Hence needs to be avoided every time.

.

5. Lead By Example

Like Lewis Cass says, ' People may doubt what you say, but they will believe what you do.' Most people in any organize would like to follow the leaders there in because that is the safest way for them to exist without taking blame.

How to become a leader is very simple. Just be the first to do the task assigned. The rest of the team will automatically join you. To your amazement you will find that everyone else is contributing and you are the least doing the job. That's how leaders motivate people.

As a result, you will gain tremendous respect with in your team and thus negative politics can be avoided, efficiency improved and productivity ever increasing.

The best is he who calls men to the best. And those who heed the call are also blessed. But worthless who call not, heed not, but rest." **Hesiod, 8th Century B.C.**

Communication Through Body Language

Part 1

The wound caused by fire heals in its time; But the burn seared in by an inflamed tongue will never heal.

Thirukural : Verse 129

Human beings are blessed creatures like no other. Apart from having a tongue to speak, we are also blessed with other organs in our body through which we can express and communicate our thoughts and feelings. We use our smile to appreciate efforts. We cusp our fist to show our anger. We wink, nod, hold our chin, crackle our fingers, yawn, frown and so on. All of these actions are being used a medium of communication to express our joy, sorry, anxiety, surprise or simply just as a routine expression.

What is communication ?

The best definition of the word "communication" I have come across is, "Communication is a systematic process in which individuals interact with and through symbols to create and interpret meaning."

Systematic means there is a methodical approach which is more of scientific in nature.

It is a **process** because the system establishes some fundamentals which deals with the ongoing changes that occur during the course of interaction.

Interact means, it could be one person sending a message to another person or a group. It could also be a Sender sends a message and receiver interprets and gives feedback.

Symbol means representation of something. Symbols can be verbal or non verbal.

There is a funny story on communication. A man and his wife had been arguing all night, and as bedtime approached neither was speaking to the other. It was not unusual for the pair to continue this war of silence for two or three days, however, on this occasion the man was concerned; he needed to be awake at 4:30am the next morning to catch an important flight, and being a very heavy sleeper he normally relied on his wife to wake him.

Cleverly, so he thought, while his wife was in the bathroom, he wrote on a piece of paper: 'Please wake me at 4:30am - I have an important flight to catch'. He put the note on his wife's pillow, then turned over and went to sleep.

The man awoke the next morning and looked at the clock. It was 8:00am. Enraged that he'd missed his flight, he was about to go in search of his errant wife to give her a piece of his mind, when he spotted a hand-written note on his bedside cabinet.

The note said: 'It's 4:30am - get up.'

"The single biggest problem in communication is the illusion that it has taken place." Says Sir George Bernard Shaw.

Communication is a tricky business especially when comes to dealing with patients in our optical industry. You are bound to use medical terminology like Myopia, Astimagtism, Polarization, Giant Pappilary Conjuctivitis, Cataract etc. In order for us to ensure that the patients understand their problem, it always better to demonstrate or use illustrations or props.

When I want to explain myopia or astigmatism to patients in my clinic, I always have a football and a rugby ball in my clinic. To show the difference between polarized and non-polarized lenses, Maui Jim used the parrot board as a demonstration. Likewise, you may use visuals, videos, or whatever comes handy to explain about the products or problems. Smart phones are very handy these days to load pictures and videos which add great value to our sales propositions. The 'touch and feel' of the products will have a significant impact on the customer's mind.

Showroom managers should take up the responsibility of imparting training and education to their staff as to how they could simplify this process so that the customers could understand the benefits of products you offer. In retail showrooms, most customers spend an average of fifteen minutes in the outlets to select and purchase the products. In which case, we need to follow the 8 Cs of communication skills as mentioned below :

Clear Objective

Have a clear objective and also ensure that key messages stand out. For example, I would like to talk to you about "Anti Reflection Coating "

Concise and Simple

Use the K.I.S.S format i.e Keep It Short and Simple so that even a lay man can understand what you say. Such as " Anti Reflection coating reduces reflection from bright light, reduces eye strain, gives you comfortable vision and makes you photogenic"

Complete

Share the message in complete manner. Otherwise, it will be ambiguous and misleading.

Consistent

Consistency in messaging develops reliability in the mind of the customer. For eg. "The products will be ready to delivery on coming Saturday morning at 10 a.m." See that you are consistent in keeping up your promises to the customer.

Correct

Correct means that it is audience-centric. In other words, you focus fully on your audience and your message fits them. Here you want to be thinking about audience knowledge levels, background, experience, requirements, and so on.

As an example, there was a senior sales manager from a Vision care company who was giving a presentation. Roughly 20 slides were prepared, and of the information shared did not co-relate to the product and the intended market.

Confident

If you are scared of putting your ideas across to customers or if you don't deliver your message in a confident way, then chances are you won't get your desired outcome. Lack of eye contact, nail biting, scratching the head are some actions which indicates lack of confidence.

Courteous

Most customers do not know to explain their problem. For eg. " I am not comfortable with the lenses that you have offered". Be courteous enough to know more about the problem by digging deep and asking opened ended questions. For eg. " What do you mean by saying you are not comfortable. Would mind to explain ?"

Checked

Is your communication error-free? Ensure, what you have said is right.

I will discuss with you more on this topic in the next issue. In the meantime, for those who plan to visit MIDO this year, have a great business trip. Ciao!

" Without communication, there is no relationship. Without respect, there is no love. Without trust, there is no reason to continue". **Anonymous**

Communication Through Body Language

Part 2

"Just as treasures are uncovered from earth, so virtue appears from good deeds, and wisdom appears from a pure and peaceful mind. To walk safely through the maze of human life, one needs the light of wisdom and guidance of virtue". **Buddha**

By the time this article appears in the next edition, Eyezone magazine would have completed 10 years since it was published. My association with Eyezone and its team begins right from the day the light of wisdom envisioned its Chief Editor which he joyfully shared with all of us. And thus, we all shared his vision, jumped into his boat to pursue the task of educating, empowering and being the source of enlightening the thousands at large in our industry. Therefore, there is every reason to rejoice this moment of accomplishment. Viva! Eyezone.

This article is in continuation of the previous piece written in the last edition on communication.

In addition to our speech, conversation and skilful use of language, we got to realize that our body communicates a lot more information by way of our dress, our warm smile, firm handshake, trimmed hair cut, clean-shaved face etc.

As Deborah Bull says, *"Body language is a very powerful tool. We had body language before we had speech, and apparently, 80% of what you understand in a conversation is read through the body, not the words."* This was amply substantiated by Albert Mehrabian through his research in 1967 in which he notes that the total liking from our communications happens as below :

- 7% happens in spoken words.
- 38% happens through voice tone.
- 55% happens via general body language.

Therefore, non-verbal communication plays an important role in our day to day life. Needless to say, this can be effectively used in our sales propositions.

The study of body language is a full grown science today. Scientists at the International School for Advanced Studies of Trieste, Italy, believe gestures as means of communication are deeply ingrained in humans.

So whilst the power of language is extremely important **to convey the right message**. The power of body language however, might be the determining factor of **how someone** makes us feel.

There are also other sub categories of Body Language such as Oculesics, Haptics, Proxemics, Chronemics,

Oculesics is the study of eye-related nonverbal communication which focuses on deriving meaning from eye behavior.

I have seen quite a few times that optometrists and sales people do not effectively use their eye contact to communicate the sales proposition. This indicates lack of confidence to the customer and hence the loss of faith in the sales proposition. Eventually resulting in loss of sales itself.

For example, if you would like to propose carbon fiber frame to your customer as the most corrosion resistant and 70% lighter than steel, you need to say that with a straight look into the customer's eye rather looking at the roof or at the carpet. If you could say that with a smile and a pleasing tone, that's a lot better.

Haptic communication is communicating by touch. In Gulf, this is only advisable between same genders ie. male to male or female to female. Otherwise, it has a danger of being interpreted as assault.

Optometrists can gently touch both sides of head of the patients to adjust their position when placed on chin-rest. A sales person can let the customers feel how soft the contact lenses are. Apart from this, a gentle hand-shake or a hug is very much a part of greeting to build our rapport which Arabs appreciate.

Proxemic communication is about the distance you maintain while speaking to the other person. **Edward T. Hall**, the cultural anthropologist who coined the term, emphasized the impact of proxemic behavior (the use of space) on interpersonal communication. There needs to be a reasonable distance of at least four feet while you communicate with you customers. Unless there is a necessity to share an important information or the clinical needs like while using a retinoscope, keep yourself at the recommended distance so that your customers can be comfortable rather being so close that your customer feels intimidated.

Chronemics is the study of the use of time in nonverbal communication. As a communication tool, Time can be used in many ways, from punctuality, to expectations around waiting and response time, to general principles around **time management**. If some customer is in a rush to the airport and wants to repair his rimless spectacles in ten minutes, you may rather not commit to him if you are not in a position to finish the job in the expected time.

In most cases of failing to deliver in time, I have noticed an error in judgment while committing deliver dates without anticipating the time lag. This is one area the store management can look into and improvise. That is to say, you probably can add one more hour or a day or a week so that when the customer comes to pick up the merchandize, he/she finds it ready for collection rather than being asked to come again.

As Stephen Covey puts, "We have such a tendency to rush in, to fix things up with good advice. But we often fail to take time to diagnose, to really, deeply understand the problem first…This principle is the key to effective interpersonal communication." Let's use our body to work it out. You can!

"Tell me and I forget, teach me and I may remember, involve me and I learn." **Benjamin Franklin**

Customer Preferences and Choices
Hermann Whole Brain Model - Part I

William Edward Herrmann, was an American researcher known for his research in creative thinking and whole-brain methods. He is considered as the father of brain dominance technology.

In 1970, after his graduation in Newyork University, he took up the assignment as Manager of Management Education at General Electric (GE). His primary responsibility was to oversee training program design; that is to monitor individual's productivity, motivation, and creativity.

In 1978, based on his research on individual 'genius' of a person, his thinking style and learning preferences, he propounded theory of stable brain quadrants which in another words called the Herrmann Brain Dominance Instrument (HBDI).

In this issue, we shall discuss Hermann Brain Dominance and how it can be used as a tool in growing our sales.

Hermann Whole Brain Model

The Hermann Whole Brain Model is a powerful tool describing the differences in information processing and thinking between individuals. Based on neuroscience research into how the brain actually accomplishes tasks, the Hermann Whole Brain Model is very useful in understanding about yourself and the customers whom you deal with.

The first step in reading a customer is to get some sense of how he or she thinks and processes information. As a brand ambassador, the more you know about the customer's thinking preference, the more effective you will be at communicating value and changing the purchasing behaviour.

Understanding your customers' thinking preferences will help you in the following ways to :

- Prepare effective sales propositions for your customers

- Adapt your communication to have the greatest possible impact.
- Collaborate with your colleagues/ optometrist in addressing their needs
- Develop a stronger long term relationship.

In the same way that individuals have right handed or left handed preference, researchers observed that different people have different strengths and areas of preferences in their thinking.

Some people are fact and data oriented. Others are detail oriented and meticulous in arranging things. Some see the big picture but have aversion towards too much detail. Whereas others are packed with emotions and relationship oriented.

The Herrmann Whole Brain Model helps us to effectively handle customers once we understand their brain dominance.

The Four Quadrant Model

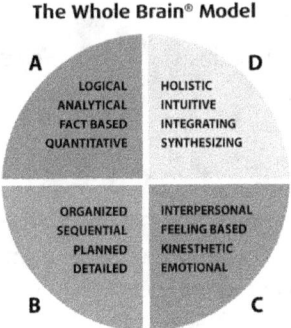

You might have been aware about Brain Hemisphere Dominance. That is for example, left-brain people are more organized and systematic. Right-brain people are more creative and intuitive.

In Hermann Whole Brain Model, the brain can be divided into four quadrants. The upper two are cerebral in character and represent the higher thinking functions. The lower two are limbic in character and represent the mammalian brain.

- The upper left (Blue) represents – Factual, Analytical
- The lower left (Green) represents – Organised, Planned, Detail Oriented.
- The upper right (Yellow) represents – Intuitive, Creative
- The lower right (Red) represents – Emotional, Relationship Oriented.

Let me give some hilarious examples.

A curious child asked his mother: "Mommy, why are some of your hairs turning grey?"

The mother tried to use this occasion to teach her child: "It is because of you, dear. Every bad action of yours will turn one of my hairs grey!"

The child replied innocently: "Now I know why grandmother has only grey hairs on her head."

How would you categorize this child's brain dominance – analytical or Blue Quadrant is it?.

Here's another one.

A police officer fixed a radar to flash at the speeding motorists. One day, the officer was amazed when everyone was under the speed limit, so he investigated and found the problem.

A 10 years old boy was standing on the side of the road with a huge hand painted sign which said "Radar Trap Ahead."

A little more investigative work led the officer to the boy's accomplice: another boy about 100 yards beyond the radar trap with a sign reading "TIPS" and a bucket at his feet full of change.

What do you think about these kids.. creative.. that means falling in Yellow quadrant.

Mental Preferences

We are all whole brained and well connected within ourselves with little bit of access to every quadrant. But along with this massive interconnection, there is a bit of mechanism with in us which helps us to pick and choose, suggesting the right direction to go.

This results in some people to go for detail and some to look for the bigger picture. Some are very emotional while some are stone faced but always keeping themselves safe from risks.

Smart sales people read and understand their customer's thinking preferences well and they adapt their messages accordingly so that they able to match these thinking styles.

We shall discuss more at length about adapting Hermann Whole Brain Model in our sales propositions in our next issue.

Until then keep thinking.

> *Thinking is the hardest work there is, which is probably the reason why so few engage in it.* **Henry Ford**

Customer Preferences and Choices
Herrmann Whole Brain Model - Part II

The greatest of woes come from not knowing contentment, the greatest of faults come from craving for gains. **Taoist Lao Tzu**

In the previous edition, we had discussed about the mental preferences of human beings and how the Herrmann Whole Brain mechanism helps people to pick and choose and suggest the right direction to go.

In this edition, we shall continue to discuss about Herrmann Whole Brain Model and its application in our sales propositions.

Herrmann Whole Brain Model – Key Points

Let us remember that like we have our own thinking preferences, customers too have their own thinking preferences too.

• Our thinking preferences influence how we see the world, communicate, make buying decisions and sell.

• There are no "right or wrong" preferences. Rather, we need to understand our strengths and adapt to the challenges.

• People who have similar preferences communicate best with each other.

• Most individuals are multi-dominant and their thinking preferences can change and expand over time. For that reason, it is a good idea to use the whole brain model with flexibility.

• In most cases your dominant mental preference will prominent in crisis situations.

How can you identify your customer's thought process?

While communicating with the customers, you need to notice theie language pattern and identify the 'verbal clues' so that you can categorize customer's thought process.

One way of detecting what thinking style your customer belongs to is to listen to what kind of questions he / she is asking:

Some Examples

Rational	Experimental
Asks "WHAT"	**Asks "WHY"**
• What about the technological innovation?	• Why is this "cutting edge" treatment?
• What is the mechanism of action?	• Why should I switch to new technology?
• What was the total number customers involved in this study?	• Why is this Contact Lens better than spectacles?
• What are the clinical results?	• Why did the old concept fail ?
Safekeeping	**Emotional**
Asks "HOW/WHEN"	**Asks "WHO/HOW/ WHAT"**
• How safe is this new contact lens?	• Who will benefit most ?
• How does this photo chromatic lens provide comfort?	• How will people see when I wear this model?
• How do I choose these two brands?	• How it will enhance my image?
	• Is there anything expensive?

How To Interact With The Customers

Most of the time, the atmosphere in a retail showroom remains challenging where we need to treat every customer differently according to his/her tastes and preferences. Therefore, it is needless to say that a lot of training and planning is required to manage our frontline sales.

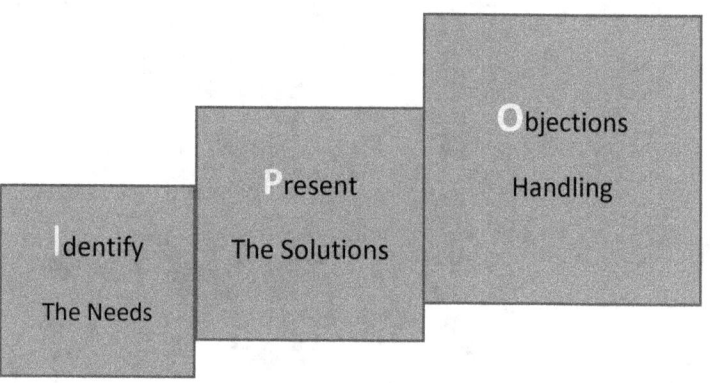

These are four thumb rules to follow:

1) Listen carefully before you talk
2) Follow the **IPOD** method
3) Telling is not selling
4) Cross-check your understanding

Identifying the Needs

Remember that in a retail store, as we witness most of the time, a customer hardly spends about 10 to 15 minutes to see, touch, listen, understand and make his decision to purchase the product. Therefore, the process of identifying the needs has to factor-in this short duration and optimize the available opportunity.

In this case, it is vital to break the ice with a smile by asking " How may I help you Sir ?" and move forward with open-ended questions such as "In order to offer you sunglasses (or frames or contact lenses) matching your needs, would you mind if I ask you some questions". This polite way of seeking customer's permission goes a long way in building your rapport with him/her at the very beginning itself.

You may proceed to understand the real need for the use of the product by asking " Where would you be using these sunglasses. Is it for regular use or on the beach or for driving etc ?" and you may go beyond to know more and more about the customer's needs so that you can offer the best product matching his taste, lifestyle and the environment he would use it.

The key steps to follow in the IPOD model while identifying the needs are

- Break the Ice
- Seek Permission
- Open-ended questions

As I had stated in an earlier article, man's mind is a composition of needs and desires. His wants are infinite in variety and number. It is only left to the inquisitive person on the frontline to crack the needs and able to match them with the best products he has on the shelf.

We shall continue to delve in the IPOD process in the coming issues and see how best we can utilize it to grow our selves along with our business. Ciao!

In each of us there is another whom we do not know.

Carl Jung

Customer Preferences and Choices
Herrmann Whole Brain Model - Part III

Be careful of excessive oaths in a sale. Though it finds markets, it reduces abundance **Prophet Muhammad**

During winter time in Arabian Gulf, it gets colder. Especially places like Kuwait and Riyaz reach freezing temperatures. People, residents and visitors alike, are changing their preferences from wearing cotton clothes to woollen sweaters, leather jackets and pashmina mufflers.

Customer preferences change out of necessity more often than their extravagance. Before we continue our discussion further about Herrmann Whole Brain Model, its about time I share some humor with our readers. I had not done it for a long time, though.

During the course of a job interview, candidates were given to analyze the below scenario and asked about their wisest choice.

You are driving down the road in your car on a wild, stormy night, when you pass by a bus stop and you see three people waiting for the bus:

1. *An old lady who looks as if she is about to die.*
2. *An old friend who once saved your life.*
3. *The perfect partner you have been dreaming about.*

Which one would you choose to offer a ride to, knowing that there could only be one passenger in your car? Think before you answer. Most people have a huge dilemma while answering this question.

1. *You could pick up the old lady, because she is going to die, and thus you should save her first.*
2. *Or you could take the old friend because he once saved your life, and this would be the perfect chance to pay him back.*

3. *However, you may never be able to find your perfect mate again.*

The smart candidate who go the job had no trouble coming up with his answer, replied.

'I would give the car keys to my old friend and let him take the old lady to the hospital.

"I would stay behind and wait for the bus with the partner of my dreams.'

Sometimes, we gain more if we are able to cross connect different quadrants of our brain.

The IPOD Process and Its Mechanics

In the earlier edition, we had discussed about how to break the ice with your customers and start the conversation by seeking their permission to have adequate knowledge about their needs.

After having all the required information to pinpoint exactly what the customer really needs, you may now proceed to discuss the solution that you may offer to your customer to match his/her requirements.

Always remember not to over-estimate the intellectual capacity of your customer. More importantly, the available time that your customer offers you to deliver the solution. Therefore, do follow the key points while you resolve their issues

- Keep it simple
- Be Specific and to the point
- Follow FAB (Features, Advantages and Benefits)
- Time Bound (No lecturing)

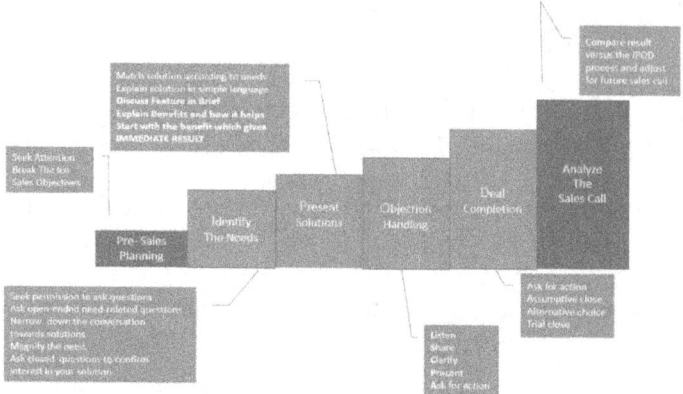

Segmenting The Customer

By now, before offering your solution to the customer, you must be having a fair idea about customer's needs, lifestyle, daily routine, thinking style etc.

→ Determine which thinking style your customer belongs to. This will help you to communicate with him based on his thinking style.
→ Recall from your memory, the current products the customer is using and align your products accordingly.
→ Position yourself with Competitive Differentiation and match customer's needs effectively.
→ Determine what might be the most common issues that arise from your customer's current competitive product use. This will help you to position your product benefits in an adequate way.
→ Highlight the new features, latest technologies, its popularity and other customers' feedback.
→ Prepare for potential objections.

Now, you are set to go. Go ahead and deliver the solution.

The Champion In You

I vividly remember one of the quotes of Muhammad Ali, the greatest heavy weight champion in the history of boxing, since my adolescence which I cherish to this day.

He said, " *To be a great champion you must believe you are the best. If you are not, pretend you are.*" That said, I do not want you to live in a fairyland where everything can happen by waving the magic wand.

Let me quote you Muhammad Ali again. He further went on to say "*Champions are not made in gyms. Champions are made from something they have deep inside them: A desire, a dream, a vision. They have to have the last minute stamina, they have to be little bit faster, they have to have the skill and the will. But the will must be stronger than the will.*"

I now leave you alone to ponder over this. Let the heat inside you make you feel the warmth and help you embrace the winter. Have a wonderful new year 2016!

We will open the book. Its pages are blank. We are going to put words on them ourselves. The book is called opportunity and its first chapter is New Year Day. Edith Pierce

Customer Preferences and Choices
Herrmann Whole Brain Model – Final Part

For everything there is a season, and a time for every matter under heaven: a time to be born, and a time to die; a time to plant, and a time to pluck up what is planted; a time to kill, and a time to heal; a time to break down, and a time to build up; a time to weep, and a time to laugh; a time to mourn, and a time to dance; a time to cast away stones, and a time to gather stones together; a time to embrace, and a time to refrain from embracing.
Ecclesiastes 3:1-8

Spring is the season of new beginnings and it comes knocking on our door. Flowers bloom to spread their fragrance. Farmers plant their seeds with hope. Butterflies dazzle to decorate. Sparrows enjoy their courtship early morning. A kind of positive energy flows through the land only to encourage people to go out of their house to shop, dine and dance. And thus we have customers in our stores.

They wear, they tear, they ask, they probe, they search for new things, check for prices, look for guarantees, eventually keeping us busy throughout the day. Spring time rejuvenates the shopping season after a brief lull due to winter.

Why do customers raise objections ?

A perfect sale in a perfect world is when the salesperson identifies the needs of the customer and offers the best solution to the need and the customer does not raise an objection. But on a routine day we come across so many objections which we are bound to handle skilfully. No matter even if we present a Tanzanite found in Mount Kilimanjaro placed perfectly on an 18k ring designed by Armani, there has to be some objection raised to satisfy the ego.

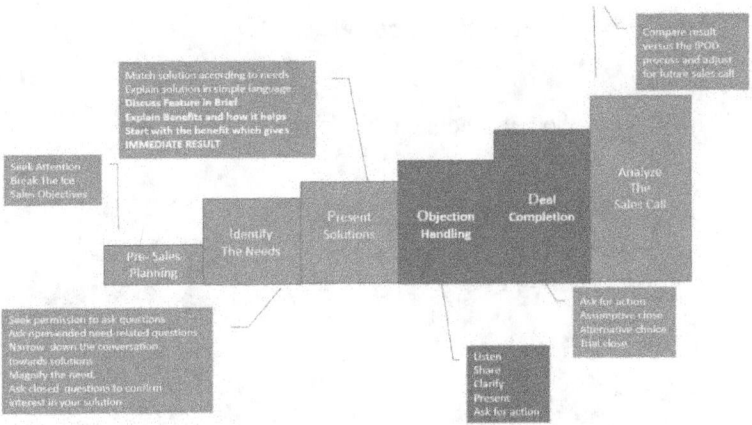

In the real world, customers frequently raise objections and these objections can take many forms. It could be due to quality, or price, or shape of may be different color.

Fortunately, this isn't as complicated as it sounds, since most sales objections are caused by one of the following:

- ✓ Customer does not believe your solution provides enough value.
- ✓ Customer is reluctant to make a change.
- ✓ Customer has a need that doesn't align with your solution.

Handling Objections Through IPOD Method

The IPOD method of handling objections is explained as follows :

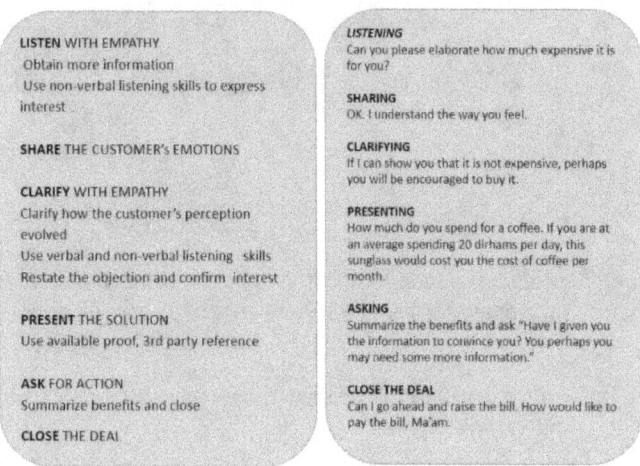

With this article, we have come to the end of Herrmann's Whole Brain Model series. I have tried my best to adapt this model to customer's thinking styles in optical stores. Perhaps I did justice to make you understand some of the many benefits that include:

- Improved communication, problem-solving, and decision-making.
- Elevated performance and customer engagement.
- Increased thinking agility and diversity within your store.

I wish you all success and hope you had benefitted from my thoughts. Raise the bar of your goal and prepare for the giant leap. On your mark, get set, GO!

" The day the Lord created hope was probably the same day he created spring" **Bernie Williams**

The Leadership Game

And how education and training contributes to it

As the leader, so the generation; as the generation, so the leader.

(Talmud Yerushalmi) Arachim 17a

Last month while I was Kuwait, my friends invited me for iftar. During the course of the Iftar, I was asked about my views on training and Continuing Education Programs and the response it generates in our Gulf markets. I delightfully shared my personal experiences with the rank and file. Before we discuss further, let me narrate this story about the king and his magnificent suit.

A pompous king was persuaded by mischievous tailors that a 'magnificent' and extremely expensive suit they had produced for him can only be seen by clever people.

In fact there was no suit at all, so when the king had worn the suit, he was actually exposed without any clothes on..

The king, then the king's courtiers, and eventually the crowds at the next royal parade, were all tricked into agreeing that the king's suit was wondrous, even though the king was bare.

No one dared to speak the truth hence no one appeared to question the claim.

So an entire population was persuaded to adopt a completely false belief - based on fear of embarrassment and reluctance to be a lone voice of disagreement.

Finally, it took the courage of a small boy who loudly pronounced the king needs to cover his modesty and exposed the sham.

Now its time to call a spade, a spade. During the course of my discussions with the owners of optical showrooms about importance of education and keeping their staff up-to-date about various products and new technologies, I was amazed by their apathy towards sending staff for training. When I had asked them who their best optometrist or sales staff was, they had spelled only a few out of the whole bunch. In fact, I had expected everyone in their organization to be well-trained and well equipped. Thus, no wonder to see these days that most of the optometrists and sales staff are below the expectations of the market in terms of product knowledge, service and after care.

If the owners and managers would like take a Red-Face Test, here is the way forward. Pick three branches and ask your staff in each branch three questions related to three products in the showroom viz A Sunglass, a Spectacle Frame and a contact lens brand. Ask your staff to give three benefits for each of them. You will be surprised by the response of even the most senior staff whom you had thought as the best. We all must admit that the Gulf optical market is way below standards needed for the optical industry to reap rich benefits like United States or Europe.

The situation however is not so dispiriting and pessimistic as it seems to be. I am glad to see companies like Johnson and Johnson, Alcon & B&L are doing pioneering work to train the opticians. Eyezone having tied up with Brien Holden is the icing on the cake. Every bud take its course of time to bloom. So does every effort. Its worth sowing the seeds of education in this barren land. As Krishna put its in Gita, *"Do not let the fruit be the purpose of your actions, and therefore you won't be attached to not doing your duty"*.

Knowledge Quotient

Someone had precisely put the mantra of leadership, " *Know before others would know. Do before others would do"*. I recently played an IQ game on the Facebook. To my surprise I scored 128. I had played something of this sort a decade back and the score was far less, honestly. I attribute my progress towards overcoming my weakness in mental math. That point I am trying to stress here is, when I had identified that my Knowledge Quotient in Math was less, I started to work on it and thus I achieved the desired result. Let the leadership ladder in the organizations be based on Knowledge Quotient in addition to trust-worthiness.

These are the steps the top management should follow :

a) **Create a Grooming Center** : A Department Head supported by a group of facilitators who are result oriented. This Core Group should not only have sufficient knowledge and experience in the related field, but also have adequate temperament to handle staff who hail from different nations and cultures. I mean someone who could differentiate between Noodles and Spagetti or Humus and chutney. They look the same but are so different.

b) **Have Short Term Objectives** : Short term objectives should help to achieve short term sales goals in the branches. These goals need to be Product as well as Port Folio specific. For eg. Imparting of knowledge about Photo Chromic lenses should increase sales in overall photochromic lenses as well as a particular brand which you might be interested to grow.

c) **Have Assessments and Rewards** : Internal assessment would give an indication of the staff's performance and its impact on the sales growth. Sharing of results with the staff and monitoring their growth on a periodic basis has resulted in evolution of think-tanks in many multi-nationals organizations. A think-tank helps a company to divide its risks during decision making processes especially when it braces the tempests of time.

d) **Hire an External Evaluator** : An External Evaluator would add credibility to the exercise. A certificate from an external institute would add great value to the credentials of the candidate and results in enhanced confidence which in turn would boost sales, increase trust in the organization and swell the leadership prospects. More importantly, the top management can have an independent assessment of their staff without any prejudice.

I have spoken my heart out now. Either you start putting this idea into action and let your genre wake up to a new dawn or continue to look towards the other way where the sun sets. Choice is yours, my friends.

***Those** people who develop the ability to continuously acquire new and better forms of knowledge that they can apply to their work and to their lives will be the movers and shakers in our society for the indefinite future.*

Brian Tracy

Dare to dream

So much has been heard and said about a word that springs myriad feelings quite often. Scholars of past, present and future love to articulate their mastery of language by expressing their esoteric inferences on this word, 'Change'.

Be the Change.

Change is Inevitable.

The only thing that is constant is Change.

Change your thoughts or you change your world.

But all through the history if you notice, Change has been the result of Struggle. Every creation in the universe even before the Big Bang had to face struggle to exist, co-exist and survive thus producing Change as an inevitable effect so much so as it was the cause.

But in order to bring about a positive change, one bearded man in the East of India, known as Rabindranath Tagore and revered as Guruji, professed the fundamental ingredient of change; - "**Chitto jetha bhoyshunyo**", meaning "**Where the mind is without fear**".

As he sowed the seed of a fearless mind, he followed suit to pave the way for its struggle to sprout and produce its green-shoots. He wrote, " Where the mind is led forward by thee into ever-widening thought and action'.

Five decades later, in another corner of the world, those green shoots had grown to become the Cyprus trees enhancing the ambience of Lincoln Memorial in Washington when Michael King, whom we know as Martin Luther King Jr, cried " I have a dream".

" With this faith, we will be able to hew out of the mountain of despair a stone of hope." He hoped against hope. " With this faith, we will be able to transform the jangling discords of our nation into a beautiful symphony of brotherhood", he envisioned.

Thus the struggle became constant ever after.

Dreaming Is Your Birth Right

The first secret of dreaming is to dream big. Dream beyond your capacity. Dreaming is your birth right which none can violate and snatch from you. As Marcus Aurelius says, *"Dare to Dream big dreams; only big dreams have the power to move men's souls."*

All self-made achievers in the world have dreamt wonderfully and fantasized voluminously. Thus they were able to map their mind, set the goals and put an action plan. And this resulted in their financial independence. Those who did not become financially independent were non-starters. Because they simply did not try. In essence, they simply did not dream or imagine what they wanted to be.

All men dream, but not equally. Those who dream by night in the dusty recesses of their minds, wake in the day to find that it was vanity: but the dreamers of the day are dangerous men, for they may act on their dreams with open eyes, to make them possible. **T. E. Lawrence**

Khaironomics – The Religion of Business

Two incidents had a profound impact on me last week which reaffirmed my faith in humanity. In fact they echoed the importance of altruism to be placed on top of any measurable service parameter. I learnt and reflected that, 'going the extra mile' can become a norm than exception, a habit than customary benevolence.

The first incident was revealed by a gentleman on the linked.in which goes as follows :

Today I went to buy a blanket in cloth market; I saw an old man was looking for same. The shopkeeper was offering it for Rs.2000, to which the old man replied he can pay only 1700 because that is what he had. The deal could not take place. The old man left disappointed. As he was about to cross the road, I felt bad and rushed to catch hold of him. As I neared him, I said, "Janab, the shopkeeper is asking for you and has decided to give you at 1700, please take your blanket". I went near the salesman and secretly slid Rs. 300 in his pocket. The sales man understood and gave the blanket to the old man for Rs.1700. Thereafter, the shopkeeper gave me another blanket at Rs. 1700.

There is an ancient wisdom, " Do good and throw it into the sea". It means the sea happens to throw back its content to the land. Likewise, all righteousness you do, will come back to you some time or the other.

The second noble deed was initiated by someone who belongs to Eye Zone itself. I am deliberately changing the names of the characters to honor the tradition and respect their feelings of keeping their charitable acts concealed.

Ali Reza is an honorable person respected by all. More than the respect he enjoyed among his friends and colleagues, he cherished with delight the very spirit that God had given him to be selfless go extra length to help those who are in dire straits, those who get entangled in the labyrinth of life.

Thus came to him the case of Fathma, a teenage girl, residing in the remote village of Kuwait. Fathma hailed from a Bedouin family, culturally less exposed to the outside world. Hence spoke little. That too in her native language, Arabic. She had been bestowed with all heavenly beauty except for her eyes. She had acute Keratoconus. Doctors diagnosed it as Acute Corneal Hydrops.

Corneal Hydrops is an uncommon complication in people with advanced Keratoconus (cone shaped cornea). She was termed legally blind and therefore cannot be treated in Kuwait. Ali Reza studied the case using his optical background. He could not digest the fact that a beautiful lass like Fathma was deprived the right to see Arfaj flowers and the Hudhud pecking the tree trunk in her backyard. He consulted his friends who advised him to send her to Singapore National Eye Center for Penetrating Keratoplasty . Lo and behold! Fathma could not leave Kuwait because she did not have her passport. Let alone paying for the air fare and the cost of the operation. Ali Reza became restless, sleepless and vouched for himself to find a way out.

And he did. It took some time though. As fate would have it, he met some officials in Red Crescent to talk about low vision remedies, the cause which he is passionately involved in and happened to mention the case of Fathma. It was as though a miracle waiting to happen. Red Crescent wondered where he had been all these days. The rejoiced at the opportunity of changing some one's life. They picked up the threads from there and absorbed all the cost of air travel including arranging for the passport and the operation itself.

Did we hear before, " One small step of a man, a giant leap for mankind". Fathma is a changed person now. She can now see and touch the beautiful Afraj flowers in her backyard and chase the

Painted Lady butterflies. But for Ali Reza, he is now looking beyond, sleepless and restless as usual, committing himself to other sublime objectives of life.

Khaironomics – What does it mean.

Khaironomics is a portmanteau word I had made of combining Khair and Economics. Khair is a commonly used word in Arab countries including India and Pakistan which denotes *Righteousness*, Goodness or wellbeing. Economics as you know is the science behind Business. In this article I am trying to emphasize the importance of righteousness in business and to what extent one should go in establishing this virtue for the benefit of our customers, suppliers and the societies we live in.

So what is righteousness or Khair ?

Going by the dictionary, it is any behavior which is morally justifiable. " There are two kinds of men: the righteous who think they are sinners and the sinners who think they are righteous", says Blaise Pascal. So whose righteousness shall we follow?

To make it simple, let follow these steps

Faith

- Believe that all good acts beget good results. If not now they may perhaps come later.
- Believe that possibilities are here and now. Develop a hunger for them.
- Believe that you have been chosen to lead to solve every customer's misery.

Behavior

- Do the righteous deeds even when no one is watching you.

- Be simple, approachable and amiable.
- Prepare yourself to absorb shocks. People with problems come to in distress.
- Conduct business fairly. At times you might have to bear the loss to see the smile on your customer's face

Compassion

- Be genuine while caring for others
- Empathize with people during communication
- Look at people's eyes while they share their problems
- Always work out interim solutions while you work out for long term solutions.

Customers' rights as well as expectations are gaining prominence day by day. Loads of information on the internet has led the consumers to educate themselves on their rights and whom to approach for redressal. Khaironomics reverses the process. In this case, you are already superseding the issue by being the best of best. You are raising the bar from being a consultant to a personal advisor. All it needs is your Will. Insha Allah, Khair.

Where there is righteousness in the heart, there is beauty in the character. When there is beauty in the character, there is harmony in the home. When there is harmony in the home, there is order in the nation. When there is order in the nation, there is peace in the world.

APJ.Abdul Kalam

Khairomics – Philanthropic Responsibility in Eye Care Business

" *We need business to understand its social responsibility, that the main task and objective for a business is not to generate extra income and to become rich and transfer the money abroad, but to look and evaluate what a businessman has done for the country, for the people, on whose account he or she has become so rich*", these are the gentle words of Vladimir Putin whom Russia has rewarded with a fourth term for Presidency.

Deepa who is seven years old represents a miracle. She lives in the village of Tarkuhat in the Lamjung district in Nepal. Deepa's family is poor. In fact, they are amongst the very poorest in this remote region. Her father earns by playing music at the local bus stop in Kathmandu. His livelihood depends on the generosity of the travelers who reward him for his performance.

One fine day, Deepa's vision deteriorated and so did her father's. Deepa knew her father had to work very hard so that she and her brothers could go to school and the fact that it was becoming increasingly difficult for him motivated her to work harder in class. Despite her best efforts, her grades fell. Her eyes were failing her. "It was getting harder and harder to read the books."

After a while she couldn't play with her friends after school any longer because she kept tripping or bumping into things. Gradually all color seeped out of Deepa's life.

When Deepa heard at school that an eye camp was coming, her heart leaped. Maybe the eye doctors would be able to help them.

The eye camp that Deepa and her family attended was in the area, but still half a day's walk away, which was hard on the family. But they did bore the pain. It was worth it. Doctor Indraman, who examined them, said that Deepa and her father suffered from cataracts and that they would receive quick surgeries in the eye hospital in nearby Pokhara, for which they would not have to pay. Their surgeries went well and

Deepa is now able to enjoy the greenery. Her scores in the class have been outstanding. There are millions of cases like this in the world that can be dealt with on a day to day basis.

The Eye Man

The Giant in the art giving eye sight has been Brien Holden. In the words of, Kovin Naidoo, interim CEO of the Brien Holden Vision Institute at the University of New South Wales, "Professor Holden was a humanitarian, a researcher and an entrepreneur". He came to be called The Eye Man. Professor Holden's <u>most recent research involved the alarming increase in eye problems in children</u> due to excessive use of electronic devices and a lack of time outdoors. Even though he has left us for his heavenly abode, all of us in the vision correction business owe him a lot for his contributions. Be it IACLE (International Association of Contact Lens Educators), APCLEP (Asia Pacific Contact Lens Educational Program), Brien Holden Vision Institute (BHVI), Optometry Giving Sight (OGS), his contributions are voluminous and awe inspiring.

Brien was a visionary and an amazing communicator. When Johnson and Johnson introduced its first silicon hydrogel contact lenses in the form of Acuvue Advance with Hydraclear, I was introduced to his institute's studies on the silicon hydrogel material which were astonishing since the amount of oxygen than can be transmissible through the material was close to 100%, greatly reducing corneal complications. Today Silicon Hydrogels make-up over 50% of the world's contact lens market. Brien was truly a contact lens pioneer. No wonder Brien Holden Vision Institute (BHVI) is unsurpassed in their accomplishments in eye research, public health and education, benefiting millions of people worldwide. It is heartening to note that Eye Zone has tied up with such a shining star that we can foresee Professor Brien's legacy will pervade and illuminate people's lives in the Middle East.

Corporate Philanthropic Responsibility in Optics

" As I see it, there are two great forces of human nature: self-interest, and caring for others. Capitalism harnesses self-interest in a helpful and sustainable way, but only on behalf of those who can pay. Government aid and philanthropy channel our caring for those who can't pay. But to provide rapid improvement for the poor we need a system that draws in innovators and businesses in a far better way than we do today", say Bill Gates.

Optics being a huge market in the middle east and more than 50% of the local population which needs vision correction in the Gulf of Arabia, I am pained to see not enough has been accomplished by the corporates in terms of education, training and serving the needy. Most of the contributions have from the governments though. It is high time the companies realize this and allocate their budgets towards this cause.

Various researches done throughout the world suggested that **"Children are TWICE as likely to be short-sighted than 50 years ago: Too much screen time and a lack of daylight 'may be to blame".**

For what concerns Philanthropy as such, Gallup reports that only <u>32.5% of U.S. workers</u> are engaged due to lack of Philanthropy. Engaged workers means increased job satisfaction, lower turnover rates and higher performance. Furthermore, according to the 2015 Giving in Numbers report, a study that <u>examined the corporate philanthropic endeavors</u> of 271 of the world's largest companies from 2012-2014, found the impact of societal investment was positively correlated with financial performance. So what are you waiting for ?

I've always said that the better off you are, the more responsibility you have for helping others. Just as I think it's important to run companies well, with a close eye to the bottom line, I think you have to use your entrepreneurial experience to make corporate philanthropy effective.

I am sure this book will make a difference in your life and in your profession from now on. Happy dispensing.

Today you have the opportunity for a great experience. Today you have the undeniable chance to really live.

It is up to you to take advantage of that opportunity. It is up to you to make the most of this day, and to live the great, unique experience this day offers.

Perhaps you'll conclude that there are too many problems keeping you from experiencing a great day, yet that would be an unfortunate mistake. For even in the face of overwhelming problems and obstacles, today can be a truly unique and positive experience

In fact, those problems can play a very positive role in the great experience of this day. By working your way through whatever may come along, you build a greater appreciation for all the goodness that surrounds you.

You also build your confidence, strength and effectiveness to higher and higher levels. And that opens the doors to vast new areas of opportunity and achievement.

About The Author

The Author of this book Mushtaq Ahmed has been in Gulf for about 25 years starting his career as a Store Keeper and rising to the level of Senior Management in the renowned Yateem Group.

He had worked in Johnson and Johnson Vision for about eleven years, winning the coveted President's Award for Europe, Middle East and Africa twice for his achievements as an Sales Account Manager and as a Key Account Manager.

He has travelled extensively throughout the region and trained many Frontline Sales staff and Optometrists in fitting contact lenses.

He established his own training institute in the name of Grace and Noble Institute in Chennai.

In this book, that author has shared all his learning experiences during his tenure and hopes everyone at large will benefit immensely out of his effort.